SO-BYP-700

280.40924
R89e

131006

DATE DUE			

WITHDRAWN
L. R. COLLEGE LIBRARY

EMPTY SLEEVES

EMPTY SLEEVES

Phillip Rushing

CARL A. RUDISILL LIBRARY
LENOIR RHYNE COLLEGE

ZONDERVAN BOOKS
Zondervan Publishing House
Grand Rapids, Michigan

THIS IS A ZONDERVAN BOOK
PUBLISHED BY THE ZONDERVAN PUBLISHING HOUSE
1415 LAKE DRIVE S. E.
GRAND RAPIDS, MICHIGAN 49506

280.40924
R89e
131006
Feb. 1985

COPYRIGHT © 1984 BY PHILLIP VAN RUSHING
ALL RIGHTS RESERVED
NO PART OF THIS PUBLICATION MAY BE REPRODUCED OR TRANSMITTED
IN ANY FORM OR BY ANY MEANS,
ELECTRONIC OR MECHANICAL, INCLUDING
PHOTOCOPY, RECORDING, OR ANY INFORMATION STORAGE
AND RETRIEVAL SYSTEM,
WITHOUT PERMISSION FROM THE PUBLISHER,
EXCEPT BY A REVIEWER WHO MAY QUOTE BRIEF PASSAGES IN A REVIEW.

LIBRARY OF CONGRESS CATALOGING IN PUBLICATION DATA
Rushing, Phillip.
Empty sleeves.

1. Rushing, Phillip.   2. Christian biography—United States.
3. Clergy—United States—Biography.   4. Amputees—United States—Biography.
I. Title.
BR1725.R87A37   1984   280'.4'0924 [B]   84-2289
ISBN 0-310-28820-7 (pbk.)
Edited by Judith E. Markham
Designed by Judith E. Markham
Printed in the United States of America
84 85 86 87 88 /   2 3 4 5 6 7 8 9 10

To Granddaddy Forty-Four and Bubba
To my wife Mildred
And to my children—
Milton, Phillip, Searcy, and Phyllis Ann

Contents

Special thanks to
Reta Seawright and Miss Louise Spears.
Also to Georgia Caple for her work in typing the manuscript.

Introduction

IT'S STRANGE TO have a life with a Before and After, but that's what mine is. There's a gigantic stripe running right through the middle of my life, separating it into those two parts, like the double line down the middle of a road.

I was sixteen the day I accidentally picked up a loose power line on a Mississippi road. My best friend tried to save me, and the current passing through me destroyed both my arms and cooked him. Much of my adult life has been spent trying to make sense of that accident, for it changed the whole structure of what I was and what I could become. Consequently, I've struggled to put Before and After into a meaningful whole. This book is about that struggle.

My story is not a sad one. For though I cried, bled, and fell down, I also learned to get up and fight and win, and thus turned disadvantage to opportunity.

Mine is the story of a black man of poor and provincial circumstances growing up in America. It is also a story of the strange advantage of being both black and handicapped. In *The Invisible Man,* Ralph Ellison comments on how whites fail to see the individuality of black people

11

and insist upon seeing them only as black, something most every black in this country can attest to. But I discovered that being handicapped created its own kind of invisibility, for my own people could not get past my empty sleeves, could not see that I was still a worthwhile human being. However, to some whites I suddenly became visible for the first time; to them I became a brave and worthy individual. As my invisibility reversed in this strange way, doors that would have remained closed and bolted were unlocked.

Finally, my story is not morbid. For the After is a story of escape from the bonds of ignorance and despair, and of slow progress into the freedom of overcoming faith.

But there *was* a Before, and that period is an important part of me, essential to understanding what I became. It began two generations ago, before World War II.

Forty-Four
and
Big Momma

THE EASTLAND PLANTATION, home of ardent segregationist Senator James O. Eastland and his family, sprawled in the Mississippi Delta like a giant white hand laid on the swamp. Not even the twisting bayous or the bubbling Sunflower River disturbed its contours. The pungent smell of earth, the vast fields of cotton and beans, and the stretching yards of Bermuda and cocoa grass suffused the scene with freshness and beauty.

At the time my story begins, plantation life was all I and my family and friends had ever known. Secured away in shanties and fields, to us places like Jackson or Memphis were as distant and exotic as London or Calcutta. We rarely went more than a few miles from the fields in which we toiled from sunup to sundown and never saw any settlement larger than a village.

I can feel the plantation rhythm even now. We rose early, wolfed down the biscuits with salt pork and gravy, and then rushed to the grind. We snatched hoes methodically through grass, bent over cotton bolls and stuffed the locks into dirt-stained burlap sacks, and plodded behind ill-mannered mules who hiked their tails and expelled whatever they had last digested. We blinked, spat, wiped, and plodded on.

Our plight was sounded in gospel hymns and spirituals glorifying a Savior who seemed faraway if not absent entirely, or trolled in blues pleading to lost sweethearts. Yet no matter how we felt, the work continued—plodding, snatching, bending—under the direction of a gun-toting redneck on horseback. He sat astride his saddle with cold, unfeeling authority, rarely speaking to us. His white face commanded power that wrenched life out of us. *We* tilled the rich soil and harvested the bounty; *we* were part of the process of life and growth. We knew it, and it was part of our sanity. Yet the presence of that overseer soured our relationship to the earth, for he reminded us that our life and our work were not our own.

Not that life was all toil. We could refuse to work on Sundays provided we cited obedience to the Scriptures as our excuse. "No, sir, captain, can't work today. The Bible say the seventh day b'long to God." If we got out of work with such an excuse, we were proud of our cleverness; we had put one over on the boss man. Some even crowed that their success in this demonstrated the superiority of common sense (their kind of sense) over book sense (The Man's kind of sense). They could not understand that Saturday night and Sunday were also part of the rhythm of being owned.

Saturday was payday and passion-night. "Pick up your money, boys, and have yourself some real fun," the overseers would say. "And remember, if you keep yourselves out of the grave, we'll keep you outta jail." So we slipped away to the juke joints and sip houses where the frustrations of a week simply boiled over.

For many, Sunday was a day of recovery, not of worship. Hangovers, split lips, swollen jaws, and razor cuts were nursed back to Monday-morning respectability. Monday was The Man's day, when there would be no more fooling around with common sense. The Man dealt with facts and figures, with gallons and acres, with bales and bushels, with fertilizers and pesticides, with fuel and tractors, with mules and plowers, with productivity and schedules, with weather conditions and boll weevils, with profits and losses. In the white man's world, neither divine ownership nor common sense were allowed to interfere with profits. The next six days belonged to The Man, though he had not made a single one of them.

Yet however isolated we were in this pattern of field work and elemental sin, we were affected by the winds of change. Underneath, we

14

knew there was a different kind of life than the one immediately before us. It's difficult to say how we knew, but my generation no longer accepted absolute oppression without kicking back—though the kicking was sometimes more symbolic than real. Even in slavery days some had let it be known that certain things were intolerable and thus earned an odd kind of respect from whites. One who did this by having the courage and the pride to stand up for himself was my grandfather, nicknamed "Forty-Four."

Granddaddy Forty-Four was the only father I knew until I was eight. He was born Willie Jackson, the son of Sam and Partena Jackson, and grandson of Georgia Ann Goosby, a Georgia slave brought over from Africa. Though I knew him as Granddaddy Forty-Four, people called him by several different names. White folks labeled him "that crazy nigger boy, old Sam's son," and tolerated him mostly out of consideration for the Goosby and Tate families (the Tates were my grandmother's people). "Uncle Tom's" resented him and tagged him as a troublemaker who was going to drive his folks into an early grave. Other colored folks gave him his nickname because of his courage and pride and looked up to him as "the nigger who don't take stuff offa nobody, not even them white folks."

Once when his white boss cocked a .44 in his face and ordered him to work in the field, Granddaddy looked right down the nose of that pistol and didn't flinch.

"If you pull that trigger, Mr. Dukes, I'se gonna choke your tongue out."

From that day on Willie Jackson was renamed Forty-Four. He was the colored who backed up what he said. To the relatively well-off Tate family, he was a rebellious "no good." But he persisted and married Maggie, their lovely daughter.

The church found out about his character when they tried to turn him out for drinking. He outsmarted the accusing deacon, who happened to be his brother-in-law.

"I gotta right to face my 'cusers," he bellowed from the front of the church.

After a lot of throat-clearing, Deacon Murdock stood up. "Well, I . . . I brought the charge 'gainst you, Jack."

"*When* you see me drinkin' whiskey, Lou?"

15

"Well, I smelt it all over your breath, Jack, and I knowed from that."

"Now that's real funny, 'cause I smelt it, too. I thought all along the stink was comin' from your breath, Lou, but I didn't go 'round 'cusin' you of drinkin'."

His remarks broke up the congregation, and the charges were dropped then and there.

Later on, when he was to be drafted into the army, Forty-Four tore up his induction papers. "Let them white folks fight they own war, 'cause this here is one nigger who ain't gonna be dyin' for them," he vowed.

That particular insult to the system brought trouble. Shortly afterward, the U.S. government, neatly dressed in dark suits, knocked on the door and escorted Forty-Four off to the courthouse. It took the influence of some powerful white folks, who intervened at the request of the Tates, to keep him out of prison.

"I always gettin' in trouble with them white folks and them Uncle Tom niggers. Them durn white folks think they can do and say anythin' they durn well please to you, and them Toms don't do nothin' but go 'round kissin' them white folks' boots."

Granddaddy's aversion to field work made him a nuisance to white bosses who didn't like coloreds who didn't like fields. When I was two, Granddaddy abandoned Holmes County for the Eastland Plantation, where for three dollars a day he cared for the mules and the farm implements and finally escaped the dreaded field work. He liked the Eastlands and got along remarkably well there except for occasional run-ins with overseers.

Though loving, Forty-Four was an invincibly proud man and a harsh and uncompromising moralist. The latter was evidenced by his reaction to my career as a thief which began and ended one day when I was helping Mr. Henry, an elderly neighbor, plant potato vines.

"Be careful, Bud Doggy. Don't step on my watermelons," Mr. Henry cautioned, obviously very proud of his melon patch. By the time we had finished planting, the prospect of owning my own watermelon patch possessed me.

Mr. Henry generously offered me the leftover potato vines, and I thanked him and hurried home to plant them. But while my hands were planting, my mind was fixed on those other vines back in Mr. Henry's garden. It wasn't long before my feet were moving in the direction of his field. And a short time later my garden boasted both potato vines and watermelon vines.

The next day, a heartbroken Mr. Henry appeared at our house, complaining, "Forty-Four, I had ninety of the prettiest hills of melon vines you ever saw, but that Bud Doggy of yours came back and took eighty of 'em, even after I gave him some tater vines."

When confronted, I admitted my guilt and stammered out my explanation. But Forty-Four was not impressed. "Boy, don't you know just 'cause you want somethin' don't give you no right to go 'round stealin'? Now bring me Buddy George!"

"George" was no buddy at all, but a leather strap and a most effective instrument for instilling morality. Forty-Four had a habit of naming things special to him, and my backside could attest to just how special Buddy George was. On this occasion, with the air of a man about to do something memorable, he let George fall four times in strokes loaded with practical philosophy and psychology. Forty-Four firmly believed that if advice didn't get results, George would. "If you can't get sense through a boy's head, then try his rump" was one of his favorite mottoes.

Another time George spoke instructing me in the matter of Forty-Four's pride, was the day I besought Mr. Eastland for some new pants.

I loathed the cotton-sack britches that my grandmother had made for me. Even at the age of seven they represented all the privation and backwardness of my lot. The dingy things hung like two raggy stovepipes and made me look like a scarecrow. Though I made every excuse not to wear them, I owned only one other pair of pants, so use of them was inevitable.

I was wearing those homemades one autumn day when, suddenly, all the britches, money, and food in the world stepped out of a big car in the person of Mr. James O. Eastland. All I had ever seen or known had come from this man's land and commissary, and now he was walking briskly past where I stood with my grandfather's youngest son, Curtis. I did not get to see Mr. Eastland often, but every time I did, his clothes looked the same—fresh, bright, and pressed. How I envied his immaculate clothing!

"How are you, boy?" Mr. Eastland started to say, but I interrupted him.

"Gimme some new britches like them you got on, Mr. Eastland, please, sir." The words just tumbled out.

Mr. Eastland gave me a look of mild surprise, asked my age, and left after giving Curtis and me a message for Forty-Four. His attitude did not inspire hope. Nor did I believe he really cared enough to help me. Perhaps he was too rich, too white to worry about or understand my desperation.

But I was never so wrong—never so happy to be wrong. For next morning Mr. James O. Eastland himself appeared at the door with four pairs of brand-new pants, two for Curtis and two for me. It was one of the happiest moments of my young life, though my joy was short-lived.

My grandfather was furious. "Boy, have you lost your mind? Don't you have sense enough not to go 'round here a-beggin' white folks for britches?"

I just stood clutching the pants, unable to understand what I had done wrong or why Forty-Four disapproved.

"I gonna hafta take 'em back," he said after he had applied Buddy George to my bottom.

That was the only time I remember feeling hatred for my granddaddy. Those pants were more important than anything else I had. I was ready to fly at him with both fists.

But my grandmother changed his mind. "It ain't right to be takin' them back, Will. He was wrong to beg, but you done whup him for it. That's enough. Let him keep the britches, Will."

So he relented and I kept the pants. But I had to promise never to beg again.

My grandmother was an extraordinary woman—strong, gentle, and courageous in unexpected ways. Her name was Maggie, but because she was both grandmother and mother to me at that time, she was "Big Momma." It was my grandmother who taught me consideration for other people, and her very presence was a constant lesson in love and sensitivity. Strangely enough, though, it was an episode involving my grandmother's bravery that first gave me a glimpse of human fear and vulnerability.

Mr. Truitt, the white owner of a pecan grove, had caught two teenage boys stealing from his trees. When he threatened the two culprits with his pistol, Big Momma intervened.

"You're out of line, Maggie," he yelled at her, gesturing with his gun. "Get out of my way. I don't want to hurt you. Move, Maggie, doggone you!"

Big Momma didn't budge. She stood there with her hands outstretched, the right one signaling the thieves to stillness and the left cautioning Mr. Truitt to patience. I truly believed she was going to be shot, standing there pleading for mercy from the angry man. His aim was sure; his voice spoke with the sound of death; and his sunken gray eyes blazed with a rage that seemed beyond all understanding. Yet the moment passed and no one got hurt. Big Momma prevailed. Mr. Truitt retrieved his pecans, and the trembling thieves hopefully learned a lesson.

I certainly did, for I was shaken by the troubling reality that my loving grandmother and those boys could have been shot for less than a dollar's worth of pecans. Afterward, Big Momma said, "Bud Doggy, that's how come I teach you not to steal, 'cause it can get you kilt!" But the image of Mr. Truitt—pistol pointed, eyes blazing, voice angry—impressed me more than what she said. He was the first person I truly hated.

Forty-Four loved me and was proud of me. I knew that. He would tell folks, "This here is my oldest daughter's boy. He gonna be just like me—gonna be a great man." He thought I was so special that he likened me to a tremendously powerful white man in those parts, Mr. Bud Doggy, and that was how I got my nickname. Mr. Bud Doggy had come up from poverty to great wealth through hard work and dogged persistence. He feared no man, backed down from nothing, and his exploits were legendary. It was something to be compared with him.

Big Momma loved me, too. Thus, surrounded by the warmth and caring of my grandparents, I remained snug and secure until one chilly, bright November morning when I was eight years old.

Forty-Four rose early as usual that day, started the fire, and put on the coffee pot. But before he could get dressed, a stroke felled him. The impact of his giant body hitting the floor between the fireplace and the bed woke me from a sound sleep. I sprang up, but Big Momma was already beside him. Then Curtis. In vain we tried to lift him. Finally I had to run to the other side of the house to get Uncle Porter and Uncle Willy, Forty-Four's grown sons. Together they lifted him onto the bed.

The doctor arrived minutes after the death angel. My granddaddy was gone.

A strange new emotion jumped around in my stomach, choked my throat, and hurried me to the refuge of a nearby ditch. I squatted there for a long time, trying to cry but finding that I couldn't. Miserable and dry-eyed, a hard knot in my gut, I saw at least dimly some of the consequences awaiting me. I knew somehow there would be changes, and I couldn't imagine how life could ever be right for me without Forty-Four.

Relatives started pouring in from everywhere to mourn my grand-daddy's passing. Neighbors came, carrying steaming pots of food and pans of freshly baked pies and cakes. The old shanty overflowed with sympathizers. And still more came.

An immobilizing grief gripped us all, and in the tension the house itself seemed to sob and moan. One by one we abandoned our places and clustered against Big Momma and Uncle Porter for strength.

Uncle Porter was our fortress. His sister, Aunt Ada, wept profusely and finally broke completely in wailing desperation. Uncle Porter attempted to comfort her and the rest of us, but the strain eventually broke him, too. His tears only intensified my insecurity. I had never seen a strong man cry.

Forty-Four's sister, Aunt Bug, arrived early. Aunt Bug was fat and mean. She stayed neat, kept money, packed a pistol, and used profanity with originality and authority. I had little reason to like her. She always made Curtis and me go to bed early, and then she would sit with the absoluteness of a bale of cotton and talk and curse and laugh, a gigantic hunk of her projecting over the edge of any chair she took. Nevertheless, her face was vividly attractive—snuff-brown, smooth and full, her eyes hazel and clear with long, firm lashes that never seemed to move, and her hair was like flowing ebony. And she moved and danced with agility and grace.

The day Forty-Four died she sized things up and went to work like a she-hawk. Her short, fat arms whipped around, efficiently doing what had to be done. Her sausage fingers stabbed first at one and then another. "You, Bud Doggy, and you, Curtis, go play in the yard. And you, Ada, stop whimperin.' The rest of y'all, go to your places and stop this here nonsense." Our strong resentment of her temporarily hushed our grief.

As I stood on the porch, leaning on the post and listening to the loud talk within, I saw an old Model T coming down the road. It stopped in front of our house and out stepped a beautiful, shapely woman neatly dressed in a blue crepe dress. Her oval face was framed by a cloud of soft, coal-black hair. I sensed her urgency as she came toward the house.

"Somebody here," I announced to Big Momma, who rushed past me to welcome the newcomer approaching the steps. I watched their tearful exchange of greetings.

"C'mon here, Bud Doggy. This be Tishie, your momma."

I ventured forward and let myself be held by my unknown mother. However strained, in those first moments she was warm and accepting, but the affections and loyalty of an eight-year-old do not pass magically from one person to another. A stubborn voice inside me said, "Big Momma still my sho-nuff Momma."

Big Momma and Forty-Four were very proud of their daughter Tishie and had told me much about her. Big Momma had read her occasional letters to me, always signed "Love, Momma." Now here she was, hugging me and wiping my dirty little face.

"Momma, is Daddy comin'?" I asked. The lingering need for my father had never been so intense. When she explained that he was not coming, disappointment walked in me like another death. She sensed this and wrapped me in silent compassion.

Once inside the house, Tishie was swept up in greetings from everyone, so I slipped outside to the porch where I could reflect on what it was like to have her here. Through the window I caught glimpses of her and heard others calling her name. Finally my little chest poked out with pride. My Momma was really here!

During the time leading up to Forty-Four's funeral, Momma and I got better acquainted. Soon the strangeness began to disappear, and with it the guilt of somehow being disloyal to Big Momma. Shortly after the funeral, while the relatives were preparing for the journey home, Momma and I sat on the woodpile talking about my returning with her to her home in what she called "the Valley."

"I think Forty-Four would want you to come with me now, Bud Doggy," she said, stroking my hair as she talked.

After a few moments of silence I asked, "When you leavin', Momma?"

"Oh, 'bout day after tomorrow, I reckon."

The following night Big Momma packed my meager belongings into a brown shopping bag: two pairs of overalls, one denim jacket, two shirts, one suit of long underwear, one raggedy pair of brogans, some marbles, a homemade slingshot, and about a dollar in change that relatives had given me.

That last night on the plantation I lay awake listening to the rhythmic rise and fall of the two women's voices. They spoke of names and places unknown to me. Then I heard Big Momma say how much she was going to miss me, and Momma's gentle tones reassuring her. I lay there sleepless, eyes wide. I knew every inch of that room, even in the dark. By the next night I would be sleeping in a different place far away from Eastland and everything familiar.

We departed early the next morning. I stared solemnly through the window of the old car, reflecting on all that had happened. When I remembered that I was leaving Big Momma I felt hurt and insecure. The journey was only about fifty miles, but in my mind it was forever.

We came to what I knew must be a town, and although it wasn't much, I'd never seen anything like it before. There were neatly maintained houses, quite unlike the ones on the plantation. Some were painted in bright colors with many windows; others were fashioned impressively from red brick. Many were elaborate ante-bellum structures with spacious lawns and little concrete boys obediently holding out their lanterns. The black skin and garish clothing of these symbols of white superiority gleamed against green grass and rows of neatly trimmed bushes. Folks meandered back and forth, and I wondered if they lived in those big, beautiful houses.

"Look, Momma! Look how that boy be dressed. I sure wish I could

22

have some long Sunday pants like them he got on." I couldn't contain my enthusiasm for all the new sights around me. "What's that?" And "What's that?" I wanted to know.

"Well, that a church, and that a bank, and that a school over there. Colored folks don't come here, less they be working in The Man's houses," Momma answered wryly.

When we finally arrived at the place called the Valley, Momma pointed out how the land dipped so that it looked like a saucer. The way she talked made me think she really liked it. She told me the Valley had some of the richest land in the world, and that the owner was Mr. Buford.

"He pretty nice and know all the families living here real good." Perhaps she was trying to convince me, for I was still fearful and skeptical. It wasn't easy to walk out on the familiar.

"Granddaddy say ain't no white man nice," I insisted, holding out against her.

She frowned slightly, then went on to make her point. "Mr. Buford don't have much money, and it ain't like the Eastland Plantation or some other places. They's only twelve families here, and everybody get along real good."

At last we drew up in front of an old gabled, barn-like house with acres of open fields and stretching miles of red hills and gigantic old trees surrounding it. Before we even got out, a crowd surrounded and pressed in on the car. I peered out at them, wondering who they might be.

Momma took my hand and showed me off. "This be my son—Bud Doggy," she said to no one in particular.

I was the subject of a lot of curiosity, no doubt about it. In the midst of all the greeting, a good-looking honey-skinned man embraced Momma and then turned to me. "This must be Bud Doggy," he said, running his fingers through my hair. "Welcome home, son."

It was a much-too-casual way to meet my father. I mumbled a greeting, but I resented the situation. These new people, even the mother I had met only days before, were strangers to me. They knew each other. I was the outsider.

"C'mon, Bud Doggy, let's go meet your sister and brothers," Momma said, shaking me from my thoughts. We entered the house; its four rooms looked like huge, well-kept stalls. This was home for Momma,

23

Daddy, Grandma Rushing, Morrie Lee and Willy, my brothers, and Hattie, my sister. Somehow I would have to fit in with them and call this home, too. Naturally enough, my brothers and sister peered at me with a great deal of interest.

Momma squeezed them warmly. "I know y'all been good, ain't you?"

"Yes, ma'am," they chimed in chorus.

"And I know y'all glad to have your brother home."

"Yes, ma'am," came their reply, though all of them were too young to make much of this occasion.

They didn't feel like kin to me. Already I was missing Curtis.

A heavy-set mulatto woman, with thin hair like red wires bristling on her head, bounced into the room. This was Agnes Rushing, my daddy's mother, and immediately I liked her. It was at least one positive feeling for the day. Grandma Rushing hugged Momma and greeted me.

It seemed like everybody had missed Momma. Everywhere she went she was closely followed by the children and Daddy, as if to say they didn't want to share her with anyone new. "Lawd, Morrie," I heard her tell him, "you act like I been gone a year." His reply set her to giggling.

As they talked, I stood in the front room with my hands rammed into my pockets. Which bed was for me? There didn't seem to be room enough to go around. At Eastland, "making do" meant getting along with my grandparents. It meant homemade lye soap when there wasn't any of the store-bought kind, salt pork when there was no other meat, and bread dipped in flour gravy when there wasn't any salt pork. But in the Valley it meant sleeping three in a bed and getting wetted on more often than not. Worse than that, it meant not being quite sure I belonged.

Bud Doggy—
A Badge of Pride

DADDY BOUGHT ME new clothes. Momma enrolled me in school the Monday after our arrival. In spite of my apprehensions, my new life began to take shape. It was different, but it had its advantages.

The school was the first one I had ever seen from the inside. It was nothing more than a one-room shack, thirty feet by sixty, into which three plantations fed 150 children. All of us were handled by a single teacher whose own education probably didn't go beyond the eighth grade. My ignorance was so great that I became the "goat" of the class— at first. I didn't even know the alphabet. But my tongue and fists soon convinced the others to stop giggling at me.

I quickly learned to do well in my studies. Not that education made much sense to me then. I could not see any real need for it, but Momma insisted. As long as I did my school work, she allowed me general freedom under the strict injunction, "Don't get in no trouble."

I went along with Daddy when he hunted and fished, and I got to know him well and admired him. He was a fine hunter, moving his muscular body with grace and speed. And when he worked, he worked hard. I helped him bridle mules, saw wood, and pick cotton. He showed me how to feed the hogs, chickens, and cows and how to milk without letting the cows kick over the pail. By the age of nine my role had shifted from being an observer to being a helper, and before I knew it, I had earned the responsibility of doing all the chores myself—and wondered then if I hadn't learned too quickly.

The memory of Forty-Four, however, still affected me deeply and seemed to set me apart from the rest of my family. When I did get a break from times-tables, church, and chores, I could usually be found in the midst of a group of boys bragging about my past exploits and how bad Forty-Four was. He was my personal legend, my claim to individuality, and I did well at dramatizing him. I would hold even the older boys spellbound. Standing before them with my hands pushed down in my pockets, rocking back on my heels and spinning around occasionally, I narrated my tales of derring-do, spicing the presentation with profanities learned at Eastland and carefully practiced since then. Quickly I earned the reputation of being "that little mannish Bud Doggy who curse like an ol' man."

My reputation troubled Momma. It wasn't just the cussing. I was growing rebellious for reasons I didn't understand. One day as I was trying to slip away from the chores, she slowed me down for a talk.

"I been hearin' talk 'bout how you gonna be like Forty-Four," she said. "He was a good man, my daddy was, but he was a man with a man's mind. I loved Forty-Four, too, Bud Doggy, and wouldn't take nothin' away from you. But you ain't no man yet. Just a twelve-year-old boy with a lot to learn. So you slow down and take in what you got to learn."

At that age, of course, advice isn't usually appreciated. I had to prove myself, to run a little harder than everyone else. Forty-Four's blood was surging through my veins. I thrived on danger and excitement and took on challenges just for the thrill.

Overhanging a hollow near our house was an oak tree that needed to be chopped down, but everyone was afraid to do the job because of the precarious position the chopper would have to be in to get at it. So I decided to take the risk. I balanced myself over that gully and hacked through the eighteen inches of hard wood, risking my life for nothing but pride. Just doing it was not enough, however. I summoned my daddy to be my audience. I basked in his amazement. I didn't hear him when he told me what "a durn fool" I was to put my life in such danger. I had become a cocky kid. "That's why they call me Bud Doggy," I remember thinking—"because I'm not scared o' nothin' or nobody."

At thirteen I was virtually doing a man's work. I'd wake up before dawn, start the fire in the big front room, and make sure the wood had been chopped for the day. Then I would milk the cows and feed the hogs. It was an endless cycle of work—dirty barnyard work—and animal manure would cake on my shoes and pants. Even then I didn't like it, but it was the only occupation I had ever known a black man to have. Because of this, I accepted my abbreviated childhood and the hard work that went with plantation life. I was pleased to be of use to my momma, and proud of my own worth as a worker.

Deep within, however, I began to examine the ways of white folks, something our unwritten laws said we mustn't do. Our misfortune was clearly intertwined with the prosperity of whites who profited by our endless hard work. In a paradoxical way, we granted them the power to keep us impotent, and yet we could not cease working for them without compounding our own misery—a misery rationalized by them as retribution for Ham's indiscretion. Precisely how Ham's descendants underwent the metamorphosis from Canaanites to Afro-Americans, or how we were elected to be the bearers of Ham's burden while whites became the custodians of Shem's blessing, remained unexplained. But since no one disputed this, the Hametic doctrine stood. For me, however, it became a theological disaster. What had I to do with a God whose rule favored whites? I endeavored to hold onto my fragile conviction that there was something noble and durable about being black, and I never reached the point of wishing I had been born white. I only wished that old man Noah had stayed away from the jug.

I also fully recognized the system's capacity for cruelty. That cruelty was one of our first lessons in the lifelong process of knowing "our place." If we stayed in our place, so we were told, affluent whites would not only ignore us but would protect us from poor whites. Considering the alternatives, staying in our place seemed prudent, and we learned to do so.

But our place was not stable; it shifted with the changing moods of whites. We couldn't tell exactly which role we were expected to play

27

until we discovered which mood was in charge. Even though the considerations dictating these moods were often irrational, perhaps resulting from a marital quarrel, a lost bet, a drop in commodity prices, or a plague of boll weevils, we were still expected to behave as if the world were consistent and fair. Thus, in reality, the only way to remain ignored (and reasonably safe) was to see nothing, say nothing, hear nothing, think nothing, feel nothing, do nothing, and be nothing; to do only what we were told what to do. And I knew that, being Bud Doggy, one day I would likely get caught "out of place" and be given the nigger treatment.

So I locked onto my hatred as a miser would to his money. I didn't know if I hated because I felt my individuality being suppressed by the inequities or because I thought the hate afforded me a power that whites could never take away.

To the white folks, however, even my hatred was invisible; I was just another "colored." And perhaps their faces blended together for me, too—except for a few who stood out for a particular kindness or cruelty. Like Miss Judy Buford, The Man's wife.

I was fourteen when Miss Judy and I first clashed. I had gone to the plantation store one Sunday to get salmon for our breakfast. I knocked like I was supposed to and waited to be let into the store. Though she heard me knocking and saw me standing there, Miss Judy looked right through me as if I didn't exist. So I knocked again, this time with a little more Bud Doggy in it. She rushed to the door and, with her haughty head held high, spoke in condescending tones. "What you want, boy?"

"Two cans of salmon, ma'am." I had learned how to be polite and challenging at the same time.

"I don't have time to be bothered with the likes of you," she retorted. But she did have time to stand there glaring at me hatefully.

Underneath I knew the signals, and how I despised them. I abruptly turned and started toward the gate, muttering, "Ain't no hussy gonna talk to Bud Doggy that way!"

She chased me. "Bud Doggy—come back here, boy! Don't you ever walk away while I'm talking to you, you arrogant little nigger! Somebody better teach you your place, boy!"

I kept walking and muttering, "Who the devil she think she is? I ain't gonna be her congregation while she lowrate me."

28

Part of me knew the trouble I was getting into, but my rebellious side took charge. If I couldn't shut her up, then at least I wouldn't stand there and listen to her. So I kept going down the road, leaving Miss Judy talking to the dust.

I told my family that all the salmon was gone. My parents were in a hurry to get to church and soon forgot about the fish.

I might have gotten away with the episode except that Miss Judy's cook came over after the service to deliver his gossip. "Did you hear what your Bud Doggy did to poor Miss Judy?"

When we returned to the house, Momma pulled me aside to explain the ways of white people. Deep inside I felt both shame and confusion, some of it directed at my momma for surrendering so easily.

"Son, you gotta understand the way things is right now for our people." I had heard that story before and everything within me wanted to reject it. Why blame me instead of Miss Judy? I said to myself. Why? How come they think I ought to stand still while Miss Judy stinks all over me and then gets mad because I smell?

It was a long time before I forgave myself for not standing up to her. With brave hindsight, I kept rehearsing what my replies should have been. She was the first white adult who had turned "sho nuff" white on me, and I had let her get away with it. I remembered the fiercely proud Forty-Four and felt that somehow I had let him down.

How to get on with whites probably absorbed me more than I knew. A great deal of the time I hung around with the Lewis boys, sons of a poor, independent white farmer who lived just outside the Valley fences. I fished, swam, and hunted with them, and I would keep the turtles, possums, and rabbits which were generally regarded as "nigger food." I sold blackberries, peas, and watermelons to them. Sometimes I even worked for their parents. With no sharecroppers under them, they were poor by white standards, but were still much better off than we were. Our relationship operated on a carefully regulated hypocrisy: we were friendly as long as we weren't in town under the public eye.

"Poor white folks ain't nothin' but trouble," my father warned. I ignored his advice.

With the Lewis boys I felt some of the power of my personality among whites. I was, for instance, such an effective joke teller that the Lewises invited me to take part in their contests. The white boys liked my jokes because I told stories that were funny and different. My material and my ability had been honed by a longstanding colored tradition. The black boys traded jokes among themselves during the long walks back and forth to the field, or on the creek banks, or at the swimming holes. This banter fell into three categories: playing the dozens (lowrating one's momma); trading choice insults (lowrating each other); and joke telling. We could go on for hours, standing each other down, toe to toe, tongue to tongue, filling the air with our version of wit.

One day I joined the Lewis boys in a joke-telling contest in which all the participants except me were white. Each of us would have a turn, and the winner would be determined by the intensity of the laughter and applause.

Buck Lewis led off with a joke that implied that a colored girl's lips were the same as a cow's—and that a colored man couldn't tell the difference anyway.

The crowd laughed so hard they rolled on the ground, giving some indication of our level of sophistication. I pretended to laugh, too, choking back the anger bubbling inside me. But I had been challenged where it hurt, and I determined to defend myself.

My opportunity came a few turns later. I began, "This here pretty, young, blonde-hair, virgin girl, the daughter of a rich plantation owner . . ." and told a joke with sexual innuendo at a white girl's expense.

When I had finished, no one laughed, and I'll never forget the chill that went around that circle. I had violated some taboos; no white in that time and place would tolerate such from the likes of me. But I got away with it! I faced them down and got away with it.

Pleased with myself, I silently promised myself I was through being anybody's scared boy. Forty-Four's pride was growing stronger in me each day, and I thought how pleased he would have been at my courage.

Despite all this exaggerated pride, I was dissatisfied and restless. I was growing fast, and the little schoolroom with its fidgety kids couldn't teach me much more. If it wasn't for Momma and all the sweet-looking girls, I wouldn't have stayed there at all.

I was almost a man, or so I liked to think. I could chop more than an acre of cotton a day; pull, load, and unload three wagons of corn;

chop wood faster than a woodpecker; ride Ol' Joe the mule'; outspell, outfigure, and understand more history than anybody else in the schoolhouse. The whole countryside knew how good Bud Doggy was.

"That Bud Doggy is somethin' else," they would say. "Just like that ol' bad white man he be named after. He'll tackle anything and git it done. But don't git that stud riled up or he'll jump in your stuff."

I thought I was hot stuff, the best-known colored boy for twenty miles around. I gloried in my reputation. "I'se the best worker, period— young or old," I boasted. To prove it, I challenged those I knew were good to contests of cotton picking, corn pulling, hoe chopping, wood cutting, and ditch digging.

"Look at that crazy Bud Doggy, kickin' up dust. That dude sure be sump'n," they'd say. Eventually my reputation spread to other plantations.

Momma was always reading me stories about Booker T. Washington, Paul Lawrence Dunbar, and Frederick Douglass. I was willing to bet they were all like my granddaddy in standing up to white people. Underneath, these stories brought a dim awareness of other possibilities in life, but most of the time I was conscious of The Man and our dependence on him.

By the time I was sixteen, I began to develop insights into the nature of the plantation system. It was white, like the sheets Momma and Grandmomma scrubbed by hand on the big washboards. It was cold, like the snow that covered the Valley during the winter. It was constraining, like the barbed wire fences that kept the cows in the pasture. And it was powerful, like The Man who owned the land we worked.

How could I ever really succeed? My success only meant profit for The Man. All the things that seemed worth having—houses, land, possessions—belonged to the white people; and they didn't walk, talk, or act like me. Furthermore, they were not interested in me, would probably even be contemptuous of my hopes and dreams. I was a field hand, a colored. The most they were willing to allow was that I could develop a loyalty for the system. I was not expected to think or create. Even as a top worker I could not become a person. To them, I was and always would be a nigger.

The system was built for profit and maintained by prejudice. My parents, who had experienced the cruelty of prejudice all their lives, were now experiencing it again through an awareness of what was happening to me. Despair and shame flooded their eyes as the system devoured my hopes in the same way it had consumed theirs. They longed to protect me against the poison that would, with apparent inevitability, embitter my soul.

But the system also had brainwashed me to an extent. I really did believe that the more work I produced the more worthwhile I was, and I fought to hold onto the small piece of personhood I possessed. Mixed in with this belief was something of the John Henry and Paul Bunyan stories, a style of personal exaggeration.

Perhaps it was a mixture of this bravado and brainwashing, but I knew I must be more than the system had defined me to be. "Gonna be a man soon," I told myself.

On my sixteenth birthday, Momma said to me, "Christmas Day, we is takin' the bridle offa you for your Christmas present, Bud Doggy. We gonna unbridle you and let you go, boy."

With all my arrogance, pride, and ambition, I certainly thought I was ready to try my wings. Yet I was so provincial and ignorant that I couldn't anticipate the obstacles that lay in my path.

Christmas
Courting

AS IT HAPPENED, 1947 was a good year for the Valley. That winter there would be no growling stomachs, no elbows jutting through frayed sleeves, no heads hung in shame because of unpaid debts. Crops had been good, and colored folks had food and money.

The soft, white locks of cotton had been picked, ginned, and sold. The corn had been wrung from its stalks and stored in cribs. The alfalfa and clover had been baled into neat blocks of hay, and the oats had been reaped and sacked. Sweet potatoes now nested underground; peanuts, peas, and beans were stacked away in barrels. Smokehouses were fragrant with the smells of molasses, ham, and beef; their rafters sagged from the weight of the meat. Shelves buckled from the weight of canned fruits and vegetables. It had indeed been a good year.

Even after all the needs and obligations were met, there was money for some of our wants—a sack of North State tobacco, a can of Prince Albert, a container of Levi Garrett snuff (fifteen cents over the counter). We held our ragged wallets at just the right angle for white shopkeepers to see and envy. And we would frequently shove the money firmly back into our pockets and silently gloat over another new ability—our power not to buy.

Soon, however, peddlers from New Orleans, Jackson, and Memphis swarmed the Valley with chairs and swings, linoleum and fabrics, pots and pans. The Raleigh man came with his perfumes, hair ointments, and skin lighteners and brighteners to enchant the wives and drive jealous husbands crazy. But the lion's share of the extra money went to Sears, who had been in the Valley all year long—several hundred pages strong. The women and children had lived in the wrinkled pages of that famous catalogue in eager anticipation of the day when they could order. And order they did.

As Christmas approached, the spirit of prosperity inspired folks to go the extra mile in doing for themselves. Mothers got their young children busy sweeping yards with brush brooms while older ones scrubbed splintered floors with steaming lye water. Christmas trees were cut and decorated. Presents were hidden in smokehouses. God-fearing wives cooked sumptuous meals on wood-burning stoves, while wife-fearing husbands, trusting the cooking chores to keep their women busy, nipped at the moonshine hidden under the porch, filed down dice, and marked new decks of cards.

Special aromas filled the air. Clove-studded hams, dripping with sugary glaze; roosters, turkeys, and geese stuffed with cornbread dressing and roasted golden brown; tender collard greens simmered in hog jowl stock beside pots of freshly shelled black-eyed peas. There were cakes—chocolate, jelly, coconut, fruit, pound, nut, and Momma's special applesauce cake. And all sorts of pies—pecan, sweet potato, pumpkin, lemon, and custard.

On Christmas Eve, Momma put the finishing touches on the cooking, Daddy did last-minute shopping, and I decorated the tree. The promise of Christmas Day and my emancipation excited me. Santa Claus would not be coming to me any more, but I wanted the day to be really good for the younger kids—my sisters, Hattie, Maggie, and Isabella, and my brothers, Morrie, Willie, Tillman, and Roy. With the advent of my independence they seemed to have become part of my responsibility.

By midnight my brothers and sisters were asleep. Daddy was still in town and Momma continued her labors in the kitchen. When the tree finally shimmered to my satisfaction, I invited her to admire it. She beamed approval.

After I swept the big room clear of bits of cotton and cedar leaves and added a log to the fire, I went into the kitchen.

"I'se finished sweepin' up, Momma. Is there anythin' else you want me to do?"

"No, Bud Doggy, nothin' left now 'cept to get the toys and candy and fruit for the young 'uns."

That done, I turned in late. Snuggling down under the warmth of the heavy, old quilts, I smiled happily to myself, relishing the thought that in the morning I would be a man.

With a Christmas morning instinct, my brothers and sisters roused out of bed before the rooster crowed. "Come see, Bud Doggy, come see. Come see." I feigned surprise and soon was answering their pleas: "Fix it, Bud Doggy." "Fix mine, too, Bud Doggy." The sputtering and exploding of firecrackers announced that Christmas was beginning all over the Valley.

Before the customary Christmas breakfast, I went to meet Bubba at his woodpile. Bubba was my best friend. We had lived next door to each other since I had come to the Valley. Our personalities were complementary—mine being fiery and aggressive, while Bubba's burned steady and slow. He was a tall, handsome, well-mannered mulatto boy with red, curly hair and the strength and determination of a tiger once he was riled.

Bubba and I played together and traveled together. Beiry hunting, plum picking, fishing, girl chasing—it was always Bubba and me, side by side. At night we would sit on his porch steps or mine and talk about everything from girls to what we were going to do when we left the Valley. We spoke of someday going to some magical, far-off place like Chicago. I could always count on Bubba when I got in trouble—and he could always count on me to stir up trouble.

Today, however, we had to decide which one of our girlfriends to visit. Bubba and I always visited together, taking turns first with his girl, then mine. One of us would chit-chat with the girl's family, thus allowing the other to romance. We had our courting down to a science we thought.

Courting in the Valley was done according to certain rules, with boys usually visiting girls on Sundays. But during the festivities between Christmas and New Year's, we had considerably more freedom. Mothers were kinder, fathers more lenient, and we could steal an extra kiss or two.

Today was really Bubba's turn, since he had gone with me to see Barbara Ann the week before. But I had promised Barbara that I would see her again on Christmas Day, and that promise conflicted with Bubba's desire to see his beautiful Sally. He had the weight of the argument on his side. Furthermore, my other special interest, Diana, was jealous of Barbara Ann.

Diana was an intelligent, decent, and pretty mulatto girl who lived just up the road from us, and from the time I was fourteen and she was nineteen, Momma was sure Diana was one thing that was going to get me into trouble. Momma would watch us closely and warn me about the five year difference in our ages. In her view Diana was at marrying age and I clearly was not. Nevertheless, I felt equipped to handle any girl who came along. At that time, my masculinity was surging, and every day I strutted and crowed like a rooster, hoping Diana would take notice.

Actually, Diana was the one who had started "our thing" going. I had viewed her strictly as an older sister. Though Bubba had suggested that she like me, I never took it seriously. At fourteen, nineteen looked pretty old. Then one day as Bubba and I finished sawing wood for her woodpile, Diana eased up behind me, put her hands over my eyes, and hugged me real close. Magnificent sensations surged through me at her touch. When I turned to face her, the dreaminess in her eyes was not sisterly at all.

From then on age difference disappeared and my interest in other girls diminished. Even when I was with them, I wanted Diana. What was happening between us hung in the air as thick as the scent of Christmas pines.

After Bubba and I had set our plans for the day, I went home and joined my family around the table. Daddy, who was not a praying man, always made an exception at Christmas breakfast by saying grace. "Thank you, Lawd, for blessin' this past year and for makin' possible this here meal. Amen." Then forks and plates began rattling, roosters and hams were carved, cakes were cut, and everyone feasted. But though my body was there at the table, my mind was with some blurry combination of Barbara Ann and Diana.

Bubba and I had worked for the three previous weeks on the Home Plantation and had received three dollars for every hundred pounds of cotton we picked. I had picked over two hundred pounds each day and had earned more than a hundred dollars. Ordinarily, I would have given this money to Momma, but this year because of the general prosperity and because I was stepping out on my own, I had purchased clothes for myself, gifts for the family, and presents for special friends like Bubba and Diana. After all this spending, I still had a pocketful of money.

"You just girl crazy," Momma had said, taking a look at my new clothes. I didn't deny it.

After breakfast I sharpened up in my new togs and went to see Diana, acting like a peacock and bearing gifts. I felt just right in the new brown jersey pants I had bought and the coat Daddy had given me for Christmas.

I gave Diana her gift, a comb-and-brush set. She seemed truly pleased, and her soft smile made my stomach—or maybe it was my heart—do the hucklebuck. I stood there feeling all warm and fuzzy inside and heard Diana say softly, "I love you, Bud Doggy."

"I love you too, baby," I said and, after looking around to make sure there were no unwanted witnesses, I kissed her.

"I got somethin' for you, too," she said.

Inside the package was a blue tie-and-handkerchief set that matched my gray-blue suit jacket. With this added touch I looked even sportier than before.

I left Diana smiling by the fireplace and joined Bubba who was waiting at the gatepost.

The
Fiery Gates
of Hell

BUBBA AND I strutted along the frostbitten plantation road, our spirits high, our steps agile and quick. It was our very best Christmas, and we were filled with confident joy.

"How do, Miz. Smith. How do, Miss Lucy," both of us called out as we passed two elderly women shuffling along in our direction.

What were we thinking about that morning? It must have been girls—certainly not the state of our souls. We were both immortal and irresistible.

Bubba and I had quite opposite tastes in girls. He liked them ebony-skinned with a little heftiness, while I liked them light and slender, just like Diana. Moreover, Bubba had a different approach from mine. He was quiet and bashful, but once he got started, he was all right—at least that's what he said about his relationship with Ella and his first experience with sex. He almost broke his neck getting to me to tell me about it.

I laughed out loud now as I thought about it.

"What you laughin' at, man?"

"'Bout you and Ella."

"That ain't no badder than that Saturday night when you was on the back of that truck huggin' Miss Dora Mae, thinkin' she was Laura."

I laughed again. "Never mind that. Just think, if Sally's all-seeing grandmomma be home, you ain't gonna be getting no hugs or kisses today."

Bubba stopped and posed jauntily in his Christmas suit. "Daddy be gettin' that car he been talkin' 'bout pretty soon. Then we be showin' them who we is for real, Bud Doggy. We gonna be shootin' through them ol' roads, and them gals will be chasin' our dust."

I always walked faster than Bubba and was a half-step or so ahead of him. I had a thing about being first, and it betrayed itself even in something as simple as walking with a friend. That's why I got to the wire first.

It was lying in wait like a deadly snake, that silver wire across the road, dangling innocently from a pole. I reached out for it as casually as one might pick up a switch or chunk a stone. I closed my hand around the wire, and when I did, the fiery gates of hell broke loose and my life was changed forever.

In an instant, my body surged with electricity. I could not let go. It was as if some monstrous, flaming hand had reached down from the clouds to burn the life out of me.

Faintly, as though he were at the far end of a tunnel, I could hear Bubba's frantic voice. "Bud Doggy? What's wrong, man? What's happenin'?" Then I could feel his hands on my leg. They were firm at first, then weaker, then gone.

My soul seemed to leave my body and float above it, but some vital part of me was still anchored to the earth by a persistent *hum, hum, hum* coursing through my body.

A glimmering light shone from the edge of a fog-filled gulf that hung below me. Something seemed to call from the light. "Phillip, come over here, Phillip," the creatures called. Were they angels? Their skin was radiant through the mist. I yearned to join them. "Come over here, Phillip," the melodic voices repeated. "Come over here."

But the humming wouldn't let me go. Somehow I knew that if it stopped for a moment I would never return to my body.

Abruptly, the strangely peaceful experience ended. I opened my eyes and found myself staring into the blinding sun. It hurt my eyes. I

39

tried to lift my right arm to shield my vision, but it wouldn't move. I looked at it.

"Oh my God, my God, my God!"

I mustered the courage to look again. The flesh of my right arm had been charred away; my fingers were pinned to the top of my wrist. The arm itself was twisted in a ghastly fashion, with seared flesh shredding from the disfigured bones.

"Oh my God, my God, my God!"

My left arm was destroyed too. Parts of my left leg and toes had ugly burns. My Christmas suit, with the new tie and handkerchief, had fallen off in shreds and ashes.

I lay there engulfed in pain, spitting blood. Then I heard Bubba groan, strong at first, fading quickly, lasting no longer than the time it takes to release a breath. I turned to see his body grow stiff and still. A remarkable strength enabled me to do what had seemed impossible a moment before. Without the balance of arms I somehow got to my feet and wobbled over to him. I shook him with my right foot.

"Bubba, man, you all right? Say somethin', Bubba."

But he didn't move. His handsome body lay sprawled like a doll slammed to the ground. I watched his skin take on the ashen hue of death, and I slumped down at his side, crying. "My life ain't nothin' no more. Oh God, I wanna die too."

Dazed, I rose and moved slowly, agonizingly, to the wire—that fire-spitting murderer. *Only four more feet to go and this whole mess will be over,* I reasoned. *I'se comin' too, Bubba. I'se comin', man.*

"Bud Doggy—Bud Doggy, chil'!"

It was Mrs. Smith, one of the two elderly women we had passed a few minutes earlier. Her tone expressed the horror I was feeling as she cried, "Set down, chil'!"

I responded to her voice, perhaps because of its motherly quality, perhaps because it was human. I allowed her to guide me away from the wire. I looked up and saw compassion washing in her eyes.

"Is Bubba dead?" I asked, hoping the wisdom of her years could refute the truth. When she did not answer, I pleaded desperately, "Miz. Smith—I gonna die anyhow. Please help me! Take the heel of your shoe and help me! Ain't nobody gonna know 'bout it."

The old woman knelt like mercy, gently rubbing my head. I persisted, "It ain't worth puttin' off. Please help me. Please, Miz. Smith."

I pleaded again, "Please Miz. Smith, please help me die." The pity in her eyes told me that my plea could never be heeded.

She continued to minister comfort. "It's all right now. Be quiet, chil'. You just be quiet. Your folks gonna be here real soon. Miss Lucy done run to get 'em."

She watched and I waited, and coldness crept into my bones. I wanted to die.

Leave-Taking

I COULD HEAR my mother's voice. She was crying as she had on the day they buried Forty-Four. I could hear Bubba's father sobbing. "Bubba, Bubba, oh, Bubba." I could hear Bubba's family falling down by his body, thumping to the ground like sacks of wet cotton, moaning and crying.

My family gathered around me. Momma knelt, lifted my head and held it gently.

"Momma. Look, Momma, what it did to me." My words bubbled out through the blood in my mouth.

"Yes, yes, Bud Doggy, Momma see. But it's gonna be all right, son," she said, wiping my tears while ignoring her own.

In the tender grip of her love, at last I could cry. I wailed out my misery, pain, and fear.

The plantation truck came. They put Bubba's body on it and laid me beside him, with Momma still cradling my head. When we got home, they carried me inside and gently placed me on Grandmomma's bed.

Cold chills coursed through my body.

"Grandma, I'm cold. I'm so cold, Grandma."

"I gonna get you some covers right now. Just rest, Bud Doggy. We gonna get you warm."

Despite several quilts, the coldness crept in and settled over me.

Daddy was visiting friends several miles away, and since hospital admission required The Man's approval, we had to wait until Daddy came home to work out the details. So I lay there, my flesh stripped from my bones in several places, and listened to the sobs that filled the old house.

Rock, my dog, came sniffing into the room. He lifted his paws onto the bed and nudged my head.

"Rock, ol' boy," I said, but I couldn't reach to pet him. He wagged his tail, returned his paws to the floor, and left, head bowed as though he sensed that something was wrong. My guts screamed with pain. Beyond the pain, there was a dawning recognition of what I had lost. My mind tried to fight off the horror that came with that realization.

"Do you want somethin'? A piece of orange?" my sister Maggie asked from the doorway. I shook my head. The terrifying impact of all that had happened was setting in with the force of a sledgehammer slamming against my chest.

Finally Daddy arrived at my bed, grunting in low moans and hardly able to look at me. Once more I was put onto the plantation truck with the bedclothes wrapped around me. On the way to the hospital the folks accompanying me talked about my condition as if I were not there.

"He in real bad shape. All them ugly burns all over him. It don't look like he gonna make it. He such a young boy. If he don't die, he sure ain't gonna be no use. He better off dead."

Their talk of my imminent death was a relief. I wanted to die. The hope of death gave me a small measure of strength.

I gazed back at the sunset as they wheeled me through the emergency entrance of the Leflore County Hospital. The sky seemed incredibly beautiful, with the rosy sun hanging in a clear blue sky. I didn't expect to live to see the sunrise.

The nurses finished cutting off my clothes, sedated me, and wheeled me to a room used for patients who were not expected to live. I heard people talking in the hallway. "They takin' Bud Doggy to the dyin' room."

My mind flashed with comforting memories. Forty-Four was the

43

first and most important. I remembered how he used to leave his bed at five o'clock each morning, start the fire, put on his work clothes and brogans, drink his coffee, and step out onto the porch. He always cut a fine figure standing there—jet black, six feet tall, and over two hundred pounds. His strength was evident in every part of his great frame—his shaved head, his powerful forehead, his strong eyes, and his firm mouth. I remembered seeing him flex himself, breathing in the fresh morning air and getting a feel for the new day.

"Gotta get me a lung full of this here air 'fore all them folks and mules mess it up," he'd announce to the world in general. Then he'd come back inside, light his pipe, fetch his water jug, and prepare for the mile-long walk to the well. He would not drink from the pump near the house. "That one fit only for mules," he declared.

I loved to go to the well with him. I'd almost skip, trying to keep up with his long strides; and he'd go along as if he didn't notice me, but letting me feel important by discoursing about subjects he thought I should learn about.

On one of those early morning trips he muttered, "Folks is runnin' around so much they can't think straight."

"Granddaddy, what's thinkin'?"

He answered without breaking his powerful strides. "Well, it mean, I guess, learnin' what you is, what you wanna do, and the best way for you to do it." He smiled, proud of himself. "Yeah, that sound pretty right, don't it?"

"Yeah," I smiled back, proud of him and proud of myself for understanding what he was talking about.

"What you think 'bout takin' that old boat out on the Sunflower River and doin' a little fishin' later? I s'pect you'd be wantin' to go one of these days."

"But s'pose I fall out, Forty-Four?" I remembered that the Johnson brothers had drowned in that river a year before.

"Bud Doggy, I know you ain't scared. Scaredness is sinful. Everything God 'tended to be scared, well He didn't give 'em no brains to think with. Folks who got brains don't need to be scared."

Forty-four wouldn't want me to be scared now.

In my mind I said good-by to other people that night, too. To Momma, who had lifted my head when I was all burnt and ugly, who

44

had dried the blood from my mouth and picked up pieces of flesh that had dropped from my arms. At that moment I could feel her love for me as I never had before.

To Big Momma and her strong, gentle love, and to the tower of strength who had taken over for her when I came to the Valley, Grandmomma.

Grandmomma Rushing was not book-educated, but had a powerful knowledge that came from something inside her. She would take me out to the woods and, with a plant or root in her wizened hands, explain its many uses, from medicine to seasoning for the salt pork we ate for dinner. She was a midwife, too, and traveled all around the area helping to deliver babies. Folks also came to her for advice with family problems. I had heard her telling them about loving and caring for each other. She always read to us from the Bible, sometimes until the kerosene burned low in the lamps. The words sounded wonderful, and I could tell that most of her soul-filled advice came from that book. I also felt that the good I saw inside her had something to do with that book.

I said farewell to my sweet Diana and to my Daddy—my quiet, hard-working Daddy who was so honest that no man would check his measures after him, so scrupulous that he had once returned a purse he had found with fifteen hundred dollars in it, more money than he would ever see again at one time.

When the sedatives began to take effect, I was certain the welcome end was upon me.

My
Injured
World

WHEN I WOKE up the next morning, I was in a clean, sterile, strange place. The bright sun flashed through cracks in the blinds. It took only a moment for the shock and horror of the previous day to return. I panicked. Then my immediate physical needs blocked all other thoughts from my mind. I struggled from the bed (how I managed that maneuver still baffles me) and wobbled into the bathroom, which some indistinct figure in white had shown me the night before. It was the first time I had ever used an indoor toilet, and it seemed much too clean to mess up. I wasn't even sure about which bowl to use. The pressure in my bladder forced me to use what I later discovered was the washbasin.

As I stood there, I looked into the mirror and saw what I did not want to acknowledge. I had no arms.

In the history of the world millions have suffered a crippling accidents such as the one that had befallen me. Yet there is no comfort in that fact when it happens. It's difficult to even describe how the realization of what had happened hit me and how the recognition of what it would mean to my future developed in me.

I was terrified, of course. No sedative could counteract the sheer terror I felt. And on that first morning I came to two very definite conclusions: I would never be able to hold a girl in my arms again and I would never chop any more cotton. Sorrow and fear racked my insides like snakes wriggling in a sack. I began to cry for all the Bud Doggy that the Wire had destroyed.

Soon the people in white were hovering round. "It's all right now," they said. "You're in the hospital now. We're going to make you feel better."

Before long they moved me from the intensive care unit to a regular ward and my horror took on a kind of permanence. Throughout the next month my pain was excruciating. The current had burnt through my body and exited through my heels, leaving holes the size of thumbprints. My toes looked as if they had been jabbed repeatedly with a hot icepick. My left leg was burned from the knee to the pelvis; and as if to emphasize my reduced masculinity, the Wire had neatly circumcised me.

I needed what seemed like an endless round of operations. In a three-week period the doctors amputated what was left of my arms and did extensive skin grafting on my legs. My right arm was taken off first, directly at the shoulder joint; the left arm was severed four inches below my shoulder. Twelve times I was put under ether, but it seemed like many more.

The pain was so intense that it blocked out everything else, and it took many forms. Sometimes it jabbed and pierced sharply. Sometimes it ached dully. At times it washed over me in waves, subsiding only long enough to begin a new assault. It came in soft-soled shoes and white dresses that promised relief for a moment of surrender. At times, it was harsh and grating, a reproach to every physical sense. It woke me forcefully and caused my sleep to be fitful, like a thousand midnights. It sucked on my soul like a tick sucks blood, and it cut into my gut like a dull knife. Sometimes it grew so intense that it would finally draw its own merciful curtain of oblivion.

All my energies were summoned to do battle with the heartless invader. My body fought hard against the intrusion; my mind joined forces with my body in the raging battle, and there was little time to reflect on my plight. Whenever the pain subsided, however, the inner

47

hurt welled up again, almost as if a pact had been forged between the two. Then physical pain became psychological torture.

The inner pain would start as guilt—guilt over being alive while Bubba was dead. In later years I learned that this is called survivor's guilt and is quite common. But there are no pills to ease such guilt. No memory can appease it. Bubba had died while trying to save my life.

When his parents visited me, shame overwhelmed me. I could not shake the feeling that they, too, blamed me for his death.

I had been in the hospital a week when they buried Bubba. Late that day I somehow managed to ask, "Momma, how was Bubba's funeral?"

She told me about the large number of folks who had attended the service, shrouded in sadness. I wept, unable to wipe away my own tears.

My daddy didn't miss a single night's visit during the first two weeks, though it wasn't easy for him to get there. Because he had to hitchhike, he would come in numb from the cold, with his feet soaking wet and tiny icicles clinging to his hat and mustache. I felt I had already become a burden, an obligation operating on the guilt of others. Whether it was true or not, that perception added to my own guilt.

Eventually the general physical pain began to subside, becoming intense only when the blood-soaked bandages were separated from the raw flesh. I gradually became more aware of my surroundings.

My roommate, Jim Hobbs, was a soot-black giant with a sharp tongue. He was forty-six years old, six feet tall, and weighed two hundred pounds. The Wire had victimized him also, branding his balding head and costing him the use of his left hand. Once I had courted his daughter Betty, but had never been introduced to Jim. Now he and his family treated me with extraordinary kindness. He proved to be good therapy for me because he liked to talk about what he was going to do back at the Homa Plantation.

"I'm full up with fire now. Ain't nobody gonna lay me in no hospital bed no more. Gonna get me a good strong bottle of whiskey and get me a poker game that gonna last till next year. And some fine woman gonna sit on my lap when I get outta here. How 'bout you, boy?"

I laughed in agreement, but the laughter was hollow. Going home was something I tried not to think about. I would be an object of pity to those who loved me and an object of ridicule to those who didn't.

"I bet them folks will stare at me like some kinda freak," I told him.

But Jim Hobbs rattled on about my possibilities, making more chatter than sense, and somehow lessened the time I spent brooding and crying.

Sometimes during visiting hours his daughter, Betty, would come to my side of the room and talk to me. I felt uncomfortable when just the two of us were together, for she served as a preview of what I knew I would have to face sooner or later. I had snubbed Betty a couple of times when I'd been in town with Diana; at those times she had not seemed to be a fine-enough momma to merit Bud Doggy's special attention. Now in my humiliation I was much less than Bud Doggy and not good enough for her. At least that was the way I felt about it.

I could almost smell her pity. While she talked about what was happening back on the plantation, I'd watch to see if her eyes would stray to that part of my body where I didn't want any eyes poking around. Not even my own. I'd wait for her glance to invade the forbidden areas and grow defensive whenever I thought she might ask, "Bud Doggy, how do it feel not to have arms?"

Somehow I managed not to let Betty or any other visitor talk about my empty sleeves. I made this request in a thousand silent ways. Touchy business here, I managed to convey to them. Most people, of course, were too shy to ask directly. And when someone seemed about to break into this realm of privacy, I'd use all the defenses I had: sinking low in the bed, faking a headache, growing sullen and silent, or suddenly becoming tired. Sometimes I'd just rudely ignore them until they got the point. By looking at their eyes and the corners of their mouths, I thought I could tell where their minds were.

For three months I permitted only the doctors and nurses to enter my injured world. And though their alien hands and eyes held only professional objectivity, their invasion brought the unnerving thought that, in losing my arms, I had also lost my human dignity.

I could not accomplish the simplest private functions without their assistance. I couldn't feed myself if I was hungry. I couldn't scratch myself if I itched. There seemed no end to my humiliation. Even to urinate I had to let the nurses guide my body, and sometimes their touch, meant for healing, inadvertently became an aphrodisiac. As I fought to suppress the emotions this evoked, I felt ashamed, guilty, and frightened.

Dr. Ford, my physician and the hospital's Chief of Surgery, set me up as a showpiece of his surgical skill. His colleagues would lift the covers and poke at me, commenting on how well the operations had gone. "Look at that," they'd say, shaking their heads in admiration of the clean incisions and neat, tiny stiches. "What a fine job, Ford."

I was not impressed. Only a new pair of arms would have any meaning for me; all the rest made no difference.

My thoughts turned in every direction, slamming me about, giving no reprieve, verging at times on paranoia. Since hell-fire and brimstone religion was an integral part of plantation life, it was inevitable that I would begin to feel God was punishing me for my sins.

In the manner of a sixteen-year-old Job, I questioned God directly. "Oh God, didn't You keep that giant, Goliath, from killin' David and make them Jericho walls tumble down? Didn't You split that Red Sea wide open for them Israelite children to cross and send down bread from heaven when they was hungry? Then, God, why didn't You move that wire? Why didn't You keep me from touchin' it, or keep Bubba from touchin' me? What did Bubba do, God? Why did he hafta die?

"If You is so good, why You let me live so helpless and different from other folks? Is You gonna give me some place to hide my empty sleeves? Is You gonna sit up there with the sun and laugh at me like that fire that burnt me?"

I got no answers, no voice from out of the whirlwind. Only confusion. My skepticism grew in proportion to my self-pity.

Maybe heaven was just another plantation and God was The Man who didn't pay attention to poor young colored boys. Or, suppose He wasn't real at all. Suppose He was just another white man.

Up to this point in my Bud Doggy life, God hadn't gotten much of my attention. I was used to hearing Momma, Grandmomma, and Deacon Brown quote from the Bible, but religion was something for the older folks. There was always plenty of time ahead to make peace with the Lord.

Bubba's death and my injury, however, had forced the issue. All of this had to mean something. And since the God I had heard about was a God of punishment and damnation, my questioning eventually took the form of harsh self-examination.

"God ain't nobody for a dude to be messin' with," I told myself. If I was going to live, I would have to figure out how to get along with Him. But it wouldn't do to get holy all at once because God surely could see through that.

"Shoot, if I was God, and some dude come crawlin' to me after all this, I'd just turn my face and shake my head."

For me, God was pretty much what the pagan gods had been for Odysseus—an unwelcome force to be neutralized through cunning and strategy; a force that made demands and produced guilt but that seldom condescended to compassion and understanding.

I put myself on trial in an imaginary courtroom. I could see clearly all the times I had used my arms and hands and fingers to do wrong things. Was that why God had taken them from me, as punishment? I had broken nearly all the Ten Commandments. And if Deacon Brown was right when he said it was the intention that mattered, I had broken them all. "In your heart, if you really want to do somethin' that ain't right, it count 'gainst you the same as if you actual do it."

"Lawd, I'se in a real mess here."

Once when a neighbor had made me mad, I paid him back after dark by opening up his pasture gate and letting the cows trample his fields. I could still feel the pleasure that act had given me.

Vengeance is mine, the Lord said to me.

I had filed nicks in quarters to make a slot machine pay me back. I had mixed water and dirt with cotton to get paid for a heavier weight. I had made a mudhole in the road so I could get paid for pushing cars out of it (a strategy that, strange to say, actually worked).

Thou shalt not steal, Bud Doggy, the Lord reminded me.

A married man once wrote a letter to Diana, and I got hold of it. I tore it up in front of the man's house and threw the pieces on the ground. His wife found the pieces and put enough of them together to figure out what was going on.

51

Do not return evil for evil, the Lord commanded.

Once I pretended to be saved to win the right to walk Diana home from church. "I stood in front of all those folks telling them how You saved me," I confessed.

A liar shall not tarry in my sight, the Lord rebuked me.

I once bought a pistol and kept it hidden from my parents. I also played "the dozens" and was disobedient to my father and mother.

Honor thy father and thy mother, the Lord replied.

Then there were all those times when I looked at the possessions of others and wanted them to be mine—houses, clothes, cars, money, land. How I resented others for having more than I did!

Thou shalt not covet, Bud Doggy.

I coveted people, too. I knew it was evil to desire a woman unless you were married to her. Though my sexual sins were more fantasy than reality, I had looked at women with unholy eyes. Sometimes I had done more than look.

As I recounted my list of sins, I feared that they were more than sufficient to seal my doom. Deacon Brown had also insisted that there was no difference between big and little sins. Sins were sins, all equally bad in the sight of God, and all could send you straight to hell. If this was true, then my case was lost. I remembered Grandmomma reading something in the Bible about mercy enduring forever, but I couldn't comprehend that either. My troubled mind could only understand that I had sinned and that the God I knew was an opponent to be reckoned with.

Phantoms

AFTER THREE MONTHS, the hospital had become a haven, a safety zone in which I had some control over who would see me and who would not. I had become accustomed to the hospital staff: the cleaning women, the nurses, the aides, and the doctors. Occasionally a covered stretcher reminded me that the hospital was a place where death occurred, but even that became a familiar and comfortable barrier against all I could not face.

Physically, I was recovering. The smell of burnt flesh had gone from my room except when the bandages were changed. The skin grafts had knitted, forming scars that concealed the patches of raw, red flesh. But mentally and emotionally, I was still raw and bleeding. It was time for my mind to catch up with my body.

Jim Hobbs continued to impart his salty philosophy of women, whiskey, and gambling. He could not wait to get out of the hospital to pursue all three. Or so he kept boasting.

For myself, I was certain that no woman would ever look at me again, while whiskey and gambling were not my style. If I couldn't even enjoy the sins of the flesh, it was difficult to imagine what I could do, even if the utility company came through with a handsome settlement.

How would an armless, sixteen-year-old boy be of any use on a plantation?

It never occurred to me that I might become something other than a common laborer. Manual labor was the only work I had ever seen black men do. This was our lot in life, and it was nearly impossible for a black man to envision any other possibility. Therefore, without arms I was without value.

The future looked so bleak that I seriously considered suicide. According to Momma, though, there was no forgiveness for suicide, only an eternally burning hell. I'd had enough of being burnt. But even the thought of suicide gave me a measure of control; I could decide whether to live or die. That in itself was one of the precious few things I could decide for myself.

So I clung to my bed the way a wounded possum clings to a tree. It was both my rock and my agony. In it I suffered all my terrors and yet managed to shut out enough to endure. What did it matter that I was not the first person to suffer a terrible injury? What had happened to me was unfair. God had abandoned me. While I could not tolerate the pity of others, I soaked myself in my own.

The head nurse of the colored section was a tall, fine-featured woman with a self-assured manner—Nurse Jackson. She impressed me as being even smarter than Forty-Four. I had never seen a colored woman command respect from whites; she answered "yes" to them instead of the drawled-out "yassa" I was used to hearing.

One day Nurse Jackson pulled open my curtain of privacy and said thoughtfully, "I think it's time we had a mother-to-son talk. Your doctor says you are nearly well and can go home as soon as you can walk. So why haven't you tried to walk? Why are you afraid to go home?"

Her all-too-accurate question stabbed me. I felt that somehow she could see deep inside of me, right through the rigid exterior behind which I tried to hide my whirlwind of emotions.

Mrs. Jackson was familiar with the story of Bud Doggy, the Delta redneck who struggled so hard to escape poverty. My nickname obviously implied something about me, and she drew upon that as a challenge.

"They call you Bud Doggy, so you must be somebody special. Bud Doggy, you're a healthy human being."

I shook my head no, and for the first time my fears poured out before I was even aware I was speaking. "I can't make no livin' for myself with no arms. All I'se used to is choppin' wood, pickin' cotton, milkin' cows, and shuckin' corn. You see what I'se talkin' about? Back home I'se gonna be a burden. I'd rather be here where everybody done got use to me."

She pushed me to take a new perspective. She told me how smart I seemed to be and how I ought to respond to a challenge. There were possibilities of work and special schools. Above all else, I had to hold my head high.

"Let the world know you're coming. Let it make way for you," she challenged.

We talked several times after that. She made sense and gave me hope to rise above my depression. I decided to try. I still didn't believe it, but I sure would try.

The first task was learning to walk. My feet were leaden, my knees wouldn't bend, my body had an airy lightness without the ballast of arms and it was difficult to balance myself. But soon I was walking up and down the hospital corridors.

The other patients began to get to know me. Heads turned wherever I went; eyes followed me. This kind of recognition, tinged with awe and pity, was something I could do without. I was "the young man who lost his arms."

On Saturday night when the plantation folk came to visit, I often overheard them saying, "I just gotta see him 'fore I go . . . just gotta see what he look like." Sometimes they'd turn and comment to me directly, "You seem to be takin' it all right, though. If it was me, I couldn't take it." Actually, I was not "takin' it all right" at all.

Seeing other young fellows pass in the corridor or come into the room with girls leaning on their arms tempted my tortured mind to think they were deliberately mocking me. I would never be able to put my arm around my girl, to hold hands with her in the moonlight, to clasp her around the waist, tickle her into smiles, or comfort her by brushing her tears away. The phantoms of what-would-never-be mocked and depressed me.

There was another phantom to reckon with also. The loss of arms is a pretty obvious handicap, but the body still has to learn for itself what that loss means. The nerves in my shoulders still sent messages to my arms, expecting them to be there. My lost arms lived at my side as ghosts, built into the memory of my reflexes, trying to respond as they always had, and never ceasing to surprise me when I realized that they could not.

Many times my phantom arms would reach to scratch. If the cover on my bed worked down low, my arms would reach to lift it back. If I lost my balance, those arms would reach out to steady me. And when I was getting seven penicillin shots a day, those arms would reach out to alleviate the pain. My ghost arms never accepted the futility of their efforts. To this day they continue to seek expression.

Eating had always given me enormous pleasure, but now it became a source of frustration and embarrassment. I never got food in my mouth when I wanted it. The nurse tried to time the intervals as best she could, but how could she know how I savored my food or the process of my digestion? Drinking was also difficult, bordering on impossible, because others could not gauge my swallows. If the nurse misjudged and gave me too much, then it would spill down my chin and stay there until it was wiped away.

The simplest of actions often became major problems. Jim Hobbs would go to sleep with the lights on and I was unable to turn them off. Though I was accustomed to sleeping with no covers, I could not sleep comfortably knowing that my disfigured body was exposed to others, yet I could not cover myself. I often held my urine and bowel movements to the point of extreme discomfort just to delay, even for a few more seconds, the embarrassment of having to request the nurse's assistance. Irrational? Perhaps. But the mind is fixed to endure just so much. When that limit is exceeded, the power to distinguish between rationality and irrationality is surrendered.

Despite this, with Mrs. Jackson's encouragement, I steeled myself for the new experiences at home. My deep admiration for her and my desperate need for support gave me a childlike faith in everything she said. I even took on her expressions and attitudes. I had already changed a bit from the fieldhand who had entered the hospital some months before. There were to be many more changes in the months ahead.

Homecoming

ON THE THIRD Sunday of April, 1948, I went home. For the last time I lay listening to the little robin outside my hospital window. That bird had shared the space of my loneliness without any false sympathy. So many mornings he had awakened me to the hurtful ecstasy of being alive, to the uncertain privilege of continued existence, and to the wonder of having briefly slipped behind the veil separating life from death. Before the Wire, Bubba and I had viewed birds as useful only for food and sport. We lured them under deadfalls during snowy seasons, and at other times killed them with slingshots. Though I had never considered their lives precious, I now felt differently. This little, red-breasted bird had become to me what the dove had been to Noah.

Using my chin and shoulder stump, I pulled open the blinds to a crystal-clear day. Dew glittered on the freshly mown grass. The robin continued to sing as I admired his frisking on the rosebush.

"Hey, friend, I gotta go home today."

He was unimpressed. With his unburdened life, he sought neither my approval or rejection.

While watching the little robin, a sense of illumination inspired me.

57

It was as if I had been granted an insight beneath the surface of things. Suffering had narrowed the focus of my interest and sharpened my power of perception. At times, like strokes of lightning, flashes of insight glowed exhilaratingly, leaving me first amazed and then even more despondent. Such moments of intensity had been occurring with greater frequency. I wanted so much to seize those moments, to possess them, but I could not. They remained elusive and fragile, as ready to vanish as a wind.

I retreated to the reality of the hospital room. With my right foot I cranked the bed to a reclining chair position. I had begun to experiment with using my feet, legs, and shoulder stump in place of my arms. But the flow of people had slowed down my progress. I was not going to make a public spectacle of myself.

My thoughts were playing a game of tug o' war between the hunger only home could assuage and the desire to remain sheltered in the hospital. The unknown and the familiar had traded places. My home had now become a terrifying place. How would they react to my empty sleeves? Would they turn away in embarrassment? Or smother me in pity? Would they see me as a person or as a problem? Would I be able to shrug off the curiosity and ridicule?

And what was Diana going to think when she got a good look at what lay under the sheets? Could I keep her? Could I even dare to want her?

And how could I stand around when everybody was working?

Mrs. Henderson, a nurse, came in with my breakfast.

"Morning, Bud Doggy. Guess you must be pretty excited. Heard you were going home today. Eat your breakfast. It'll get you off to a good start."

I barely tasted the watery grits, overcooked sausage, and scrambled eggs.

"Not hungry?"

"I wanna be good and empty when I get home. My momma got somethin' special."

She went out with the uneaten food. In a minute she was back with hairbrush, comb, and mirror. She tussled the little comb through my messy, resistant hair. It had not been cut in nearly four months and had been combed so seldom that it had rolled up into tight, beady knots.

58

"Tender-headed?"

"No, ma'am." I was not ready to admit anything. But it hurt. The pitiless comb, made for white folks, tore against my hair, lost several teeth, and finally popped in two.

"I saw your girlfriend when she was here the other Sunday. She's real pretty."

"Thank you." I blushed, wishing she would end the conversation.

"What's her name?"

"Diana," I answered with resignation.

"How far does she live from you?"

"Right up the road."

"Will she be welcoming you home?"

"I—I don't know." That last question focused my mind on a possibility that hadn't occurred to me before now. Diana was just crazy enough to be standing there when I got out of the car. I wasn't ready for her yet. I wanted to evade such an encounter.

"Here, take a look."

She had finished combing my hair and putting lotion on my face. I assessed the Bud Doggy profile, the first time I had regarded myself approvingly since entering the hospital. I looked a little older and a little harder. A bit of pride stirred in me; the image was recognizably that of the old Bud Doggy, my nose and mouth still strong, and my appearance only needing a bit of attention here and there. My hair needed a better part and the budding mustache could stand a trimming. That was what the girls went for. My phantom arms reached for the comb. I retreated again.

"Doesn't that look better?"

"Yes'm," I replied, shrinking in the face of failure.

Finally it was time to say my farewells. The doctors, nurses, and patients crowded around me.

"Stay in touch, Bud Doggy, and let us know if we can help."

I was touched but wasn't articulate enough to tell them how grateful I was.

When I got to Mrs. Jackson's office, I found her sitting with pencil in hand, reviewing the nurses' reports. Not knowing how to get her attention, I just stood looking at the mountain of books and papers that filled her office. I had never seen such evidence of learning before. The sight of it strengthened the respect I had for her and awakened possibilities in myself. At last she looked up.

"Why, Bud Doggy," she said, half rising, "come in. What gives me this honor?" Her warmth instantly set me at ease.

Next to Momma and Diana, Mrs. Jackson had become the dearest woman in the world. I tried to tell her how much I appreciated what she had done for me.

With her arms around me, she walked me back to my room and then hugged me good-by.

"You're an intelligent young man, and maybe a remarkable one," she told me. "You can still live a normal life. You can be somebody if you really want to be."

I fought back the urge to cry. "Good-by, Nurse Jackson. I won't ever forget you."

"Ready to go home, Bud Doggy?"

I turned. It was Daddy.

"Yassuh!" I smiled. "How's Momma and them?"

"They all right. Anxious to see you. Told me to hurry home."

We piled into Mr. Doug's car. He was the only black man on the plantation who owned an automobile.

"Momma got a big meal for you, boy. She been cookin' all mornin'."

Daddy was not an outwardly emotional man and talked little on the way home. He was a man who found contentment in his own thoughts and was willing to let others do the same.

I was grateful for his silence and let myself be absorbed in the passive flow of scenery. Mr. Doug's old car chewed up the road between the hospital and the plantation. As we passed the Watkins' place, only two miles from home, a reluctant excitement gripped me. As we crossed over the hump of Edwards Creek bridge, we were on the plantation itself. In contrast to the sterile cleanliness of the hospital, the shanties now seemed shocking: broken windows, tin roofs, squeaking doors, grassless yards, and dust everywhere. Flies, gnats, mosquitoes, fleas, rats, and mice drifted through the filth. In the Valley it was not uncommon to battle critters for a place to be. Snakes, lizards, hogs, chickens, dogs, frogs, and birds fought for scraps of food. Being human did not quite remove you from that competition.

But today was Sunday, and Sundays were always different. The folks, as they always were on that day, were scrubbed, greased, polished, and pressed. They occupied the windows, doors, porches, and yards of the shanties where they gossiped, played, read the Bible, and courted, seeing all and being seen by all. "Too bad they can't save up all their Sundays and live them all in a row," I thought. But I had no business worrying about them when I had two empty sleeves that were actually full of my own trouble.

How was I going to do it?

The folks were wondering the same thing, of course. Their craned necks and searching eyes showed their concern as they sprinted from cane-bottom chairs, wood benches, and porch swings to get a firsthand look. I slumped low in the car to avoid the burden of their gazes.

We passed Deacon Brown's house. He nearly tripped down the steps in his zest to halt the car. Mr. Doug slowed, but Daddy intervened.

"Don't stop, Doug. Gotta get Bud Doggy home to his Momma." A mixture of pride and relief surged through me. Daddy did understand. He was trying to protect me.

When we came to within a few hundred feet of the big house, an unofficial welcoming party of farm animals and birds meandered in the road, blocking our way. They seemed to know that being The Man's property gave them immunity no black man dared to violate. Daddy left the car to herd them out of the road, his tone with them more timid than it had been about Deacon Brown. Though his gentle insistence finally won out, I felt his humiliation. We did not stand high in the order of things.

Within minutes we were in front of the big house itself, a huge, unpainted farm structure that boasted such conveniences as electricity, gas, and indoor plumbing. It sat on an expansive lawn surrounded by pecan trees, pines, and weeping willows. East of the house were rolling hills and woods of tall, stately oaks, pines, and cedars which no one was permitted to cut. The Man's orchard and gardens were luscious with peaches, pears, grapes, strawberries, apricots, and figs. Nature seemed to smile on him in a way it did not smile on us.

The car moved to the rear of the house, where, much to my dismay, Daddy said, "Stop here awhile, Doug. Miss Judy wanna see Bud Doggy." Old Doug at the wheel promptly pulled up the car. This was one stop we would have to make. I muttered under my breath, thinking back on the painful encounter with her two years before. We had managed to avoid further confrontations since that time.

"It ain't gonna be long," Daddy reassured me. "Miss Judy been askin' about you, and I tol' her we would be stoppin'." But deep down I knew the length of time we would be there would be determined by Miss Judy and The Man, not by us. I felt buck-naked, vulnerable, and helpless. No doubt this request came from her sense of obligation; I couldn't believe Miss Judy was truly interested in my welfare.

Mr. Doug announced our arrival, and Miss Judy bounced briskly to the car, trailed by her twenty-three-year-old, mentally retarded son, Peter, and The Man himself, Edward Buford, her husband.

"Good to have you back, Bud Doggy. Missed you plenty," she said.

"Yes'm," I replied, lifting my eyes to hers. Nurse Jackson had told me to do that. Facing the world meant facing white folks—The Man in particular.

When I raised my eyes, I saw a Miss Judy I had never seen. It was like seeing her with new eyes. She seemed less encompassing. But there was a more important difference. Those clear, blue-gray eyes that had been so unfeeling were now floats of compassion. Her tears startled me and I felt a momentary respect for her. Then guilt and pride intervened and smothered that emotion and I shifted my attention to Peter. I had always liked Peter and had felt compassion for him, perhaps because I never needed to use up energy fearing or resenting him. Ironically, in his retardation Peter managed to demonstrate qualities of racial fairness that the other whites in all their intelligence did not.

"Glad to see you, Peter. How you been doin'?"

"All . . . all . . . right," he said. He reached out and closed his hand around my sleeve and tugged on it with gentle innocence. Every eye there gravitated to that short, fat, white hand. Surges of shame nullified every ounce of self-esteem I had left. "Th . . . th . . . at bad," he said. I managed to nod agreement.

"He's gonna be all right, son," Mr. Buford said with the authority of a plantation boss. He nudged Peter aside and stepped closer. "We're glad to have you back, Bud Doggy. Don't be worrying none 'cause we're gonna take good care of you."

He turned to Daddy. "Take good care of this boy now, and let me know if he needs something." Mr. Buford's words lifted me a little even though I understood that they were more for his benefit than mine. Instead of being loving and kind, Mr. Buford was simply being loyal to the standards mandated by his background. He was The Man, the lord of the plantation. The inventory of his possessions included me. My strength had worked his fields, mended his fences, and harvested his crops. Now, my disability obligated his charity to underwrite my family's efforts to provide for me. Both his pride and social standing would not accept less of him. He understood the responsibilities of a person in his position. And we were fully confident that he would back up his promise. There were three things we had learned to count on in the Valley— The Man's word, boll weevils, and field work.

Mr. Buford turned back to me and repeated, "We're gonna take good care of you, you hear?"

"Yassuh," I said obediently.

Buford turned away, taking Miss Judy and Peter with him. No sooner had he left than Harold, his thirty-eight-year-old son, took his place beside the car. He welcomed me with kindness, even affection, telling me how much I had been missed at the deer camp where I had worked last year, and how sorry everyone at the camp was about the accident. The men in his hunting party had voted to buy me artificial arms; he would work out the details. I had always liked Mr. Harold a lot. He had treated me with respect. He had always thanked and paid me for the chores I did for him and had encouraged me to be diligent in my studies and morals. I had never heard him use the word "nigger," and he never asked demeaning questions about my relations with girls. But, even so, his attention now only made me feel uncomfortable.

When the white folks' welcomes were finally over, I sank back into the car, exhausted by my first real, post-hospital encounter.

A half-mile later I was home. As Mr. Doug honked the horn, the waiting family poured out of the house, down the shaky steps, over the loose brick walk, and across the grassy ditch. The yard was filled with shouts of welcome. I stepped out of the car and into Momma's arms and was ushered inside to the seat of honor, Grandmomma's old, cane-bottom rocker.

Soon, the family was seated around the table. "You just wait a minute, young man, till your Daddy give grace," Grandmomma said to Morrie, who had grown impatient and begun to eat. Thus, we began the ritual of Sunday dinner. Momma sat next to me, forking the delicious food into my mouth while also feeding herself. In spite of everyone's forced politeness, or because of it, I felt ashamed. Only babies got fed that way. We ate in strained silence until five-year-old Roy said what had been passing through everyone's mind: "Daddy, Bud Doggy can't eat by hisself." They tried to ignore him, but the little fellow repeated his observation several times. Sweat from my humiliation broke out on the back of my neck.

"Momma, I got enough now. Can I leave?"

Daddy's head shot up in astonishment, his fork suspended in mid-air. "You sure you got enough?"

"Yassuh," I lied unconvincingly. I left ham, black-eyed peas, rice, string beans, chicken, dressing, cabbage, cake, and sweet-potato pie to retreat to the room where I slept.

In the future I would have to do better than this. "Please help me, Lawd."

I spotted a short yellow pencil on the sewing machine. Nurse Jackson had told me of a white man with no arms who had learned to write with his toes. I considered this possibility. I was so absolutely defeated that it seemed necessary to accomplish something for myself. I picked up the pencil with my teeth and began to write on the newspaper that covered the machine. Perhaps it was only the concentration created by my special need, but the words "Bud Doggy" appeared with a legibility that was even better than my previous penmanship had been. I could not quite believe what I had done. I eased up, closed the door with my foot, and repeated the act. Only God knew how much this simple act actually meant to me. I wanted to shout, "I can write! I can do somethin'!" But I couldn't reveal my accomplishment—not until I had perfected it. For the time being it would have to remain a secret, a personal joy I could hug without arms.

"Bud Doggy?"

"In here, Momma."

I quickly moved the pencil back in place and dried my eyes against the newspaper.

"You all right?" she asked, recognizing that I had been crying. "Sure you all right?"

"Yes'm. I just glad—" I faltered, almost betraying my secret, "to be back home, Momma."

"I'se glad too, Bud Doggy," she said, wiping my eyes with her apron. She tenderly ruffled my hair. "You gonna be all right—but we gotta get some of this hair off, huh?"

I smiled approval. Then I followed her into the front room where the conversation of the family touched on everything but the issues concerning me. Everyone avoided discussion of my problems, and courtesy dictated that I feign interest in the current plantation gossip.

Little Roy eased over, leaned against my leg, and began exploring my empty sleeves.

"Where is you hands, Bud Doggy?"

A lump rose in my throat as I looked into his innocent face. "My arms got burned in a fire, Roy," I explained as simply as I could. "The doctors had to cut them off to save my life."

"Is they gonna come back, Bud Doggy?"

"No, Roy. They is buried up on top of the hill."

When this difficult moment had passed, I saw the approval on the faces of the older folks and understanding in those of the younger ones.

"Now, y'all go out and play and let your brother rest," Momma declared. Little Roy lagged behind the others, looking back over his shoulder.

Grandmomma broke the silence. "Did Momma tell you about the cake Diana brought?"

"Oh, yes. She was up here in the early part of the day," Momma said. "Left the cake and said to say hello."

As Momma, Grandmomma, Daddy, and I sat talking in the front room, it was suddenly clear to me that my perspective had changed. Plantation matters now barely pricked my interest. What did it matter about the cotton budding up, the chickens being hatched, what fish were biting, or what trees were bearing fruit? These familiar subjects were no longer part of my being. Such talk only reminded me of my inadequacy, of all the things I couldn't do. The issue of what I could do was still being evaded. More and more it was becoming clear that my future, if I

65

could have one, lay somewhere beyond the plantation. But I couldn't envision any prospect of my ever being able to leave the plantation to claim that future.

Just then I wanted to get back to the yellow pencil. As slender as it was, it still projected a measure of hope.

"Guess you might wanna walk 'round the house by yourself a bit," Momma said, sensing my discomfort. She seemed to know better than I did just how I felt.

I began moving about the house. In the kitchen I saw my plate of partially eaten food now swarming with flies. I stood there watching those ugly insects as they gorged themselves, frustrated by my inability to swat them away. In Grandmomma's room I looked at the bed on which I had lain on the day of the tragedy. The pain of that memory washed over me. My eyes moved to Grandpa Rushing's picture. Grandmomma had often spoken of him.

"He was a real man, your grandpa. He was a proud man, too. Had a good business head on him. Bought over three hundred acres of land before he was thirty-five, built me a house as good as any the white folks had around there, and put two children through private school. He wouldn't work for nobody but hisself."

Often she had told Daddy, "You oughtta take your money and buy your own land, boy. Your daddy would turn over in his grave if he knowed you was spendin' your whole life workin' land you don't even have the right to be buried on."

I had resolved to make her proud of me someday by owning my own land, but this thought now became painful.

Through the window I caught sight of Diana, her long, thin body in the neat white blouse and faded sky-blue skirt. Her moon-shaped face was lifted toward my window and me, as it had been so many times before the accident.

Our eyes met. I moved closer, carefully positioning myself to conceal my empty sleeves. She smiled, standing tall, and then, with what seemed to be teasing cruelty, she turned and walked away. Before the Wire this window had been one of our meeting places. Now I felt a wrenching inside. My phantom arms strained for her as she moved out of sight.

"Have you seen the beans yet, Bud Doggy? I planted them for you this year," Momma said as she entered the room.

She had caught me watching Diana. I obediently followed her out to the porch where the limas were. During the summer the beans would grow along the strings from the ground to the top of the porch. They would make shade as well as food. But what difference did it make to me now?

I was glad when the day ended. Morrie helped me remove my outer clothes. After sleep had settled throughout the shanty, I eased out of bed and made my way to the porch. There I gyrated until I managed to get my penis out of my underwear. For the first time in four months I relieved myself in private.

I kneeled right there and said my prayers. The first day had been a little better than I had dared to hope. Feeling a bit more like a person, I slipped back into bed and slept soundly.

Relearning
Life's
Basics

NURSE JACKSON'S WORDS had been both reassuring and challenging, but the reality of the daily struggle at home was frustrating and depressing. My extreme dependence made me feel both guilty and inadequate, while the new perspective I was gaining on the system fired me with anger and hatred I was unable to vent.

I despised the cotton and the fields. They sapped my Momma's hope and strength. Helplessly I watched her go to the fields each morning and return each night caked with the dust. Often I stole away to my hilly retreat on Prince Edward Hill, overlooking the fields where the folks worked. There, the sight of Momma with her back bent and her vitality dwindling was troubling to me. Cotton stalks, briars, and cockleburs raked her flesh, disfiguring her limbs with dried blood and ugly scars.

I hated The Man for profiting from her suffering; I hated Daddy for allowing her to work the fields; I hated myself for my inability to stand up for her.

I hated the folks for their apathy. I needed an example of humanity from them, some symbol of positive personhood. If such demeaning existence was their lot with both hands, what could there be for me? Their misery mirrored my own and put a distance between us. Yet my physical dependence forced me to cling close to them for security, for they were all I had.

I hated the talk about how many bales this plot would yield or how thick Daddy's syrup was. No harvest could compensate for the misery and suffering it brought; Daddy's sweetest syrup could not sweeten the bitter reality of plantation life. Nevertheless, I kept my views to myself. I had nothing better to offer them, and they needed their illusions. Besides, I lived by their sweat, not my own.

When I'd had a fill of chitchat about mules and plows and beans and oats, I would ease away to read and think. I read everything I could find, turning the pages with my chin and toes: *The Life and Times of Frederick Douglass,* Booker T. Washington's *Up from Slavery,* Dickens' *Great Expectations,* and Melville's *Moby Dick.* I also read *Reader's Digest, Life, Pittsburgh Courier, Grit,* and other local and national publications Momma got as well as novels Mrs. Harold sent down from the big house. The Bible, however, was my mainstay. I plowed through it twice, cover to cover, particularly focusing on characters who had suffered and triumphed. Many nights I stayed up until early in the morning, studying and thinking. I was beginning to believe that I might become a worthy person, after all, and not remain just a useless, disfigured hulk.

One moon-flooded night in October, 1948, after hours of reading *Great Expectations,* my stomach growled for food, urging me into the kitchen in search of leftovers. I carefully picked up Grandmomma's old brass kerosene lamp with my shoulder stump and chin. Though slowly developing some coordination with this maneuver, I had to be careful I didn't start a fire. I passed quietly through the room where the family slept and into the kitchen to discover only a little cornbread left from supper.

Though any of my family would have cheerfully gotten up to prepare something for me, I could never ask them to do it. They already had too much to do and needed their sleep. But I vowed I wouldn't go to bed hungry and defeated.

With my foot I opened the fire door of the big iron stove. Then I lifted off the eye cover and pushed it to the side, holding the eyelifter between chin and shoulder. Next I got some paper from the pile we kept for fires and stuffed it through the little door with my foot. I picked up some kindling with stump and chin and shoved it in on the paper. Next I unscrewed the top of the kerosene can, very slowly picked it up, and poured some over the papers and kindling. I put paper on top of the stove near the open eye. Holding a long match between my teeth, I lit the paper, pushed it into the stove with a piece of wood, and closed the fire door with a sigh of relief.

With chin and stump I lifted a skillet from its hook and maneuvered it onto the stove. Because I had not used my shoulder for lifting before, the skillet wobbled uncertainly. The next step was to get some grease in the skillet. I straddled the big lard can and lifted the top off with my legs. With a long cooking spoon between my chin and stump, I dipped out the lard. It would take the wood stove a while to get the skillet hot, so I put more kindling on the fire.

With the big spoon I lifted two eggs from the pail and laid them on the table. Since we didn't have a refrigerator, it was necessary to break each egg in a cup to see if it was good. I took each egg between my lips, cracked the shell, and let the contents fall into a cup. Then I poured the egg into a teapot. Somehow I broke the eggs so cleanly that no trace of the shell got into them, and none had spilled on me.

From another pail I picked up an onion and transported it to the table. I then went to the hutch, pulled out a bowl, and dipped it into the water. By holding a knife under my chin and pushing down on the blade with my stump, I cut the onion in half to make it easier to peel. Then I slowly peeled the skin with my teeth. My battle began in earnest as I stabbed at the slithering onion. I had to corner it with the knife blade while my eyes watered as much from frustration as from the onion itself, but I finally cut enough to add to the eggs. I picked up the egg pot, put it on a chair, and slid the onions from the table into the pot with a spoon. Holding a fork with my chin and stump I stirred the mixture. Then I poured the eggs from the teapot into the skillet, using the bottom of the pot to shield my face from the crackling grease.

I scrambled the eggs with the big spoon. When they were done, I covered the skillet handle with a dishcloth and slid it off the open fire.

I took a plate from the hutch to the stove and with the big spoon scraped the eggs from the skillet. Then I engineered the plate down to the table.

I took a bowl to the white clay churn by the door. Kneeling, I lifted the top off, grabbed the long-handled dipper, and tried to dip out the milk. So much sweat had built up on my chin and stump, however, that the dipper slipped into the churn. After retrieving the dipper, I tried again, this time successfully. I lifted the bowl with my teeth onto my stump and maneuvered it steadily to the table and sat down to eat eggs, buttermilk, and cornbread.

Later, I stood on the porch breathing in the beauty of the moonlit countryside and exulting in the triumph of my victory banquet—perhaps the most important meal of my life. Setting that special table somehow symbolized the turning of my destiny.

For the next six months I virtually isolated myself in the house and yard during the day when everyone was in the fields. My pride would not allow anyone, even family, to see my clumsy efforts at doing things—the awkward dipping and twisting of my body, the repeated failures in even the most fundamental tasks. But no matter how awkward or painful my methods, they were better than relying on someone else. While the family struggled in the cotton fields, I grappled privately in my own self-taught course in basic survival.

Forced to improvise, I learned to brush my teeth by sticking the toothbrush in a crack in the wall or between the door and the frame and moving my mouth back and forth; I washed my face using my chin and stump to manipulate the washcloth; I washed my ears by hanging a towel on the edge of a table or on a large hook; and to rinse, I dipped my whole face in the washbasin.

Taking a bath was really hard and had to be planned with precision. First I needed a stool beside the portable tin tub. I would then take a handtowel between my chin and stump, soak it, put it on the stool, and wash by rubbing my body against it. After that I stepped into the tub, wrapped the towel around one foot, washed one leg, then switched the towel to the other leg and finished washing the bottom half of my body. This whole process took place while I was scrunched up in a small washtub used for laundry. Needless to say, it was hard on back and legs.

No curious eyes saw my gyrating as I learned to dress myself. No one saw the stubborn sock slip away as I tried to hold it with one foot. When I got it on, I either worked it up my leg with my toes or hooked the top on a dresser knob and stretched it over my leg. Someone would have my shirt buttoned, except for the two top buttons, and laid out flat on the bed, ready for me to work myself into it. My family were good to me; they helped with those buttons, tied my tie, and combed my hair. They helped any way they could. But I didn't want them too close; the less they had to do for me, the better I liked it.

I pulled my pants on and off by means of suspenders. Suspenders were for old men and little boys and were definitely out of style, but I was willing to trade stylishness for a bit of independence. I'd hang my pants over the back of a chair and step in one leg at a time. With my left stump I'd pull up the left suspender; then I'd take the right one, still hooked over the back of the chair, kneel, stretch into it, and pull up the other side.

I learned to do chores such as making the bed, sweeping the porch, and mopping the floors; gradually this gave me a measure of pride in being able to contribute to the keeping of the household. I would fluff the ginned cotton mattresses with my foot and then straighten the covers with my chin and stump. To sweep or mop, I held the broom or mop between stump and chin and pushed it along the floor with my foot. Although Momma discouraged it, I also learned to wash clothes with my feet and did the pressing by maneuvering the iron with my chin and stump.

Nevertheless, for every success there were many failures. Car doors, locked gates—no matter how hard I tried, there was always the thorn of another humiliation, and my pride magnified my shame a thousandfold.

One afternoon when I was home alone with no one to help me, I had to go to the bathroom. Ordinarily I would have left my pants undone in case of this kind of emergency, but on this particular day I decided I wanted to be decently dressed. Desperately I struggled to undo the zipper on my pants but finally wet myself. I hid behind the smoke-house for an hour, too embarrassed to let the family see me.

Another time I was trapped for two hours in the outhouse. The path from the house to the toilet was lined with bushes so that normally I was able to use a device I had rigged up to get my pants down. After my previous experience, I had invented a device consisting of a piece of thin wire, one end of which was attached to my bedroom wall and the other end shaped into a hook. With it I learned to zip and unzip my pants. Thus, I could undo my pants in the house and walk to the outhouse unnoticed. On this afternoon, however, by the time I had finished, Mr. Banks was waiting near the woodpile for my father to come from the fields, thereby blocking my path to the house. I couldn't tolerate the thought of exposing my nakedness to him, so I sat for two hours in that stinking little building with the flies feasting on my backside. After that humiliating experience, Morrie installed a similar device for me to use in the outhouse.

And so it went from day to day. Through both humiliation and victory I picked up new methods for doing what was routine for others. My mind was the teacher and my body was the student. In time I learned to unscrew jar tops, play checkers, jump over a five-foot fence, and run. I learned to get through a barbwire fence without tearing my flesh and to climb pasture gates to hunt with my dogs. For a while I even played on the Valley sandlot baseball team as a pinch runner and umpire. Without arms, however, the players invariably heard "out" when I said "safe" and "strike" when I said "ball." Reluctantly, I gave it up.

Through it all I developed a sense that I did have a mind and a will capable of shaping my life. In a paradoxical way, my handicap enabled me to envision far-reaching, wondrous, liberating goals. Yet I was never truly joyful. Because a physical part of me was missing, I could not accept myself as a whole, worthwhile person.

Living
in the
Shadows

I WAS STILL struggling to maintain the old Bud Doggy image, one that had been a childish exaggeration to begin with and that now seemed downright ludicrous. I wasn't a special somebody; I was a frightened, miserable boy who didn't know what to make of his life. I couldn't talk about what was troubling me to anyone, but my personal misery revealed insights about other things, if not about myself.

I saw how plantation life was shot through with dishonesty. It trained us to ignore inner feelings in order to protect that very life itself. We feared the price of change more than we valued the principle of truth. We kept up images and avoided realities.

We stood silent when cruelties degraded us and called it "turnin' the other cheek." We vented our frustrations in pathetic shouts and called it "holiness." We lived in a shanty and called it a "house." We ate salt pork, cornbread, and syrup and called it "breakfast." We fathered sons, abandoned them, and called it "manhood." We gave The Man hell—behind his back—and called it "tellin' him off." We downed our misery in moonshine and called it "livin' it up." We knifed each other

74

and called it "courage." We possessed our women like overripe roosters and called it "love."

Sometimes I at least saw the truth about myself and faced it. The folks in the Valley chose not to see. They had a lifetime of practice. But their blindness further separated me from them.

Folks in the Valley were unprepared to cope with my armlessness. Though I don't believe they meant to hurt me, to them, my empty sleeves were a bold repugnancy. The emotions they suppressed in dealing with whites always surfaced when dealing with each other, and I felt the full weight of that suppression in their stares, gossip, and raw comments. "Lawd, would you look at that!" "Ain't that a pity, chil'." "I'd rather be dead than be like that."

Angered by their ignorance and insensitivity, I disciplined myself to answer innocent questions politely and steeled myself not to answer other questions at all: "Pardon me, I don't mean any harm, but how did you lose your arms?" "How do you feed and dress yourself?" "How much a nub ya have left?"

The cruelties that cut the deepest, however, were the vulgarities of lower-class white boys. Their degrading remarks about my sexuality were crude and cruel. Sometimes I successfully ignored them, sometimes not. One time, having been pressed too hard with "Hey, boy, how d'ya hold on?" I lost my temper and replied, "Now, why don't you just bring me one of them pretty little white chicks and ol' Bud Doggy will show you how."

My antagonist's face puffed like an overripe tomato about to burst. He headed for me with fire in his eyes. An older colored man pulled me out of harm's reach, explaining away my "sassiness": "That boy been half-crazy ever since he got outta the hospital. All that fire done scorched his brain. Y'all know that." Later, learning that one white man was making noises about killing me, Mr. Buford put out the word in the redneck community that I was not to be bothered.

Shortly afterward, Daddy took me aside and told me: "Son, if you take a pole and start messin' around with a rattlesnake, and just keep doin' it, it'll get real mad. It'll get so mad it'll start bitin' itself, and will keep on bitin' itself 'til it die of its own poison."

I'd always had the gift of gab, and some of my sallies were triumphant. I found I was able to deflect people or shut them off with "doctor talk" I'd picked up in the hospital. "Well, it's like this. Forceful currents of electricity consumed the vitality of both arms, necessitating bilateral amputation of the upper extremities."

When I saw how well this polysyllabic nonsense worked on colored folks, I tried it on white boys. It worked on them, too. Skin color had nothing to do with intelligence, I reasoned. But the white boys didn't want to admit that an armless colored knew more words than they did, so they came up with an ingenious theory to explain my intelligence.

"It's like this, Bud Doggy. When the doctor took off your arms, the strength from them went straight to your brain. That's how come you got more brain power than other colored folks, and it gonna keep on makin' you the smartest colored person around here."

I was so starved for acceptance of any kind that I did not bother to challenge them. Besides, they had to assert white supremacy. We were all involved in a vast game we didn't fully see or understand.

The folks attributed my "big brain" to heredity—after all, I was Forty-Four's grandson, and he was nobody's fool. But though they granted me a verbal wit and intelligence, they gave me little or no credit for understanding everyday living. Losing my arms seemed to mean that I had lost all practical intelligence. If I said a bale of cotton weighed 550, invariably I would be overruled. If we were reminiscing, my memory was always in question. It was as if they had reversed the white folks' theory and thought that my brains had been in my arms.

Though praising me for my accomplishments, they would not ask me to do the simplest tasks. If I were walking with a much younger person and passed someone who wanted a message delivered, they would always ask the younger person. Somehow they didn't believe I could kick a door shut or fetch the mail.

Everything I said or did was related to my loss. I had always walked fast, but now my gait was attributed to my not having arms to weigh me down. If a girl liked me, it was because she felt sorry for me. If we broke up, it was because she could not put up with my armlessness. If I cussed someone out or failed to talk to them, I was held to be "touchy." No matter what I did, I couldn't win.

If I got angry, it was "because of his condition." If I didn't get angry, it was "because he ain't got no arms to fight with." If someone offered me food and I declined, it was "because, you see, he 'shamed to eat with no arms." And if I refused a drink, it was "because he scare' he might git drunk an' fall."

People offered me pretzels in the same manner they were given to little children—with a pat on the head. They forced money into my pockets, assuming my need to be greater than theirs. These attitudes, of course, were not conscious attempts to hurt me. They loved me, coddled me, and gave me sympathy and credit for not going crazy. But their pity made me a sort of non-person.

In their eyes, being both armless and colored, I could never achieve any kind of personhood. They could not understand my need for self-respect, because somewhere along the way they had lost their own.

Edward Creek bustled with life. Cranes splashed in the clear, rolling water. Birds sang in the groves of weeping willows and majestic cottonwoods along the white, sandy banks. Bullfrogs leaped from rock to rock, lizards scampered over the sand, and snakes slid through the stiff grass and around the water-washed rocks.

Careful not to lose balance on the moss underfoot, I waded in the shallows and slurped the fresh water. My thirst quenched, I stretched out on the soft sand and looked up at the fleecy clouds.

I had been home from the hospital for seven months. Though my feelings had evolved through enormous changes, I was still hollowed out by grief. I could not forgive myself for Bubba's death. And I could not imagine enduring a lifetime of my own death-in-life.

The Wire had become an evil god, a demon that ruled my life and would not let me go. It had whipped me. Before I had been somebody special; now I cringed in fear, both in reality and in fantasy. I couldn't even pass under an electric wire without fear. I was constantly haunted by the specter of the Wire. Somehow it was going to find a way to mock me with an even greater hurt. Despite the reassurances of doctors, I was convinced any children I might have would be born armless. The Wire had been more effective than the plantation system in undermining my manhood. Now it ruled me more completely than any slavemaster.

The tranquil scene at Edward Creek should have been the place where I could sort through my fears and fantasies and break out of them. But even there my thoughts went round and round in agitation. Was there possibly another me, neither the Bud Doggy of the past nor the person I was now? Would some third me emerge out of this trouble? Though I asked myself these questions again and again, I found no answer.

Genuine
Hypocrisy

"TAKE IT TO the Lord in prayer," the old folks said.

Prayer did not work for Bud Doggy. Though I had grown up in an atmosphere of religion, I was a skeptic. Bud Doggy played it cool. Besides, I had plenty of reason to doubt the religion I saw around me.

Until the Wire, my most memorable encounter with religion had occurred during the autumn of my fifteenth year. At that time the Valley View Baptist Church held its annual two-week revival services. The little country church was alive each night as souls were coaxed, shamed, or dragged to the mourners' bench so that God himself could get a crack at the sinners. This was the time to get religion, renew religion, and brag on religion already gotten. It was also a time for folks who lived far apart to get together, spread their gossip, and out-testify each other.

Prior to the service, folks would mingle outside in friendly clusters and mothers made last-minute trips to the outhouse with their well-scrubbed children. When the first strains of "Amazing Grace" or some other gospel hymn led by the deacons announced that devotions were beginning, the two hundred or so filed into the little church, already tapping their hands and feet methodically, working themselves out of

79

themselves so the Spirit could take charge. In moaning undertones, half talking, half singing, they praised God, writing their own music as they went.

The harmony wafted out the windows to the small groups remaining outside. Some were teen-agers who eased away while their elders were in the grip of the Spirit. Others were boyfriends and husbands who had escorted their ladies and "had done good to come this far." Through the bushes, flickering firelight marked the spots where crap games and drinking parties were organized to pass the time. These recalcitrants would be prayed for right along with the sick and shut-ins.

The first week of revival consisted mostly of singing, testifying, praying, and acknowledging guests from neighboring churches. There was some "jackleg" preaching by men who professed to have received "the call" but who did not actually pastor a church. The most pressing business of that first week, however, was to build up to the second week—the mighty climax. The drawing card during the second week was a big-name preacher who held a host of converts to his credit. Turnout was largely dependent on the popularity of this evangelist who was expected to "preach hell outta them folks so the Spirit can do its work."

The Spirit was summoned through long, hacking prayers which some successfully converted into sermonettes. "Did you hear him slip in a sermon in the name of prayin'?" The pace and volume of the praying and singing increased until, with heads locked tightly and eyes fixed on the ceiling, the congregation gave up control of their "willfulness." Some actually reached such a state that they fainted and had to be carried out. Church was a collective possession, and within its confines folks felt freedom to lose themselves. The most bizarre behavior was acceptable so long as it could be rationalized as "being caught up in the Spirit of the Lord."

The mourners' bench, in front of the pulpit, was the focus of attention. On it sat the sinners, young and old, in varying degrees of receptivity to the Word. Some seemed nearly asleep, almost falling off the bench, only to awaken with a gut-level "Whoop," "Hallelujah," or "Amen." Some would pray. Some would even "get religion."

The sixth night found me still sitting where I had each night during the revival—on that pine mourners' bench with twenty other sinners.

Each night I had heard the same songs sung, the same prayers prayed, the same fervor summoning the Holy Spirit, and yet I remained untouched.

Until I came to the Valley, I had never heard the Scriptures read, a prayer said, or the gospel preached; I had not even seen the inside of a church. I didn't know what being "born again" was all about, and I was fidgety and more than impatient with the whole affair. I was on the bench because of Momma, who sure did think it was important.

After the first few nights, I asked Momma, "How will I know when I get born again?"

"You just stay right there on that bench, Bud Doggy Rushing, till you come to the Lawd. I ain't raisin' no sinners up for the devil. He will hafta grow his own. You'll know when it happens and won't nobody hafta tell you. The way you treat yourself will tell you, the way you treat other folks will tell them, and God will know 'cause He do the savin'."

So I sat sweat-glued to the long, hard bench night after night, listening to testimony after testimony . . .

"The Wednesday night I prayed through, I saw them angels just walkin' 'cross hell in a spider web!"

"Chil', it was early Friday mornin'. I been talking to God a long time. I told Him I was gonna stay right there till He heard me. All at onct I started feelin' light. I look at my hands and they look new. I look at my feet and they did too. Even my ol' clothes look brand-new. Then I knowed for sure that I got my religion. Can't nobody tell me nothin' 'bout being born again, honey, 'cause I knows I got religion."

"It was right before the break of dawn. I was out on the hillside just a-prayin' when this here light come and stop right over me. Then the moon start skippin' 'round. The stars went blinkin' all about. It was then I knowed the Lawd had saved my soul!"

One night, on the strength of this last testimony, I prayed to be awakened at three in the morning so I could go out to my own hillside. I did wake up before dawn, and guessing it to be about three, I eased out of bed, slipped on my clothes, and crept quietly out of the house. As I stepped onto the porch, I was amazed at the darkness. I couldn't see my hand in front of me. Fear overtook my resolve to pray; there were snakes and other dangerous things out there. I went back to bed.

As if Momma's concern wasn't enough, Diana began pushing me, too. "Now, Bud Doggy, I can't be lettin' you kiss and hug me while you is on the mourners' bench. It will just keep your mind offa God."

Then Jim Perkins started walking Diana the two miles home after the service each night. This proved to be the deciding factor. It was time to get religion and end this nonsense.

There was a definite ritual for getting saved in the Valley View Baptist Church. First you had to get off that bench. When you stood up, there was great rejoicing and craning of necks to see who just got saved. The congregation clapped their hands and stomped their feet and shouted, "Praise the Lawd" and "Thank you, Jesus." When the sinner finally sweated his way through the jubilation to shake the preacher's hand and face the congregation, he took a vow: "I will come whenever I am called and go wherever I am sent."

I made it through the first part with no problem. And only Momma seemed to know it was pure hypocrisy. She glared her disapproval. Nevertheless, I stood before all and spoke in a strong, steady voice amid the cries of "Amen, I hear you brother" and "Amen, praise the Lawd."

"Brothers and sisters," I began, "I know I got my religion 'cause the Lawd come to me today while I was all bent low pickin' cotton, and He done raised me up. He put fire in my bones. He put religion in my heart. He cut loose my froze-up tongue and made me feel new-like, free, and real, real good."

They broke loose with shouts and applause. Except for Momma.

That night Diana waited for me at the door. I stepped right up to her Bud-Doggy style, took her hand, and strolled away, winking over my shoulder at the befuddled Jim and gloating within.

The following Sunday I was baptized in the creek. There was whiskey on the preacher's breath, and I thought, "Aha. Reverend ain't nothin' either." I was worried that he would let go of me suddenly. To strangle from the water during baptism was a sure sign you didn't have religion! But I got through it without incident.

That self-interested lie was all the religion I had. Deep down, I think I was interested in the subject of salvation, but my own cleverness and conceit blocked any genuine investigation of my feelings.

Until the Wire, I lived for Bud Doggy. And after the Wire it took me a long time to make sense of religion.

Encounter
on the
Bridge

THAT HYPOCRITICAL ENCOUNTER with God had occurred the autumn of my fifteenth year. It was now another autumn and I was seventeen. I was also determined to take my own life.

My despair was complete. I was worthless. I didn't feel like a man, nor was I able to act like one. The only victories I could win were with eggs and zippers. Thus, on a morning rich in cloudless blue sky, clear cool air, and colorful foliage, I was determined to end my life.

I knew exactly how I was going to do it. My throat and chest felt tight as I headed for the bridge where I would throw myself off and end what should have been finished months before. As I walked, even the beautiful day was a taunting reminder of all that I would never do again.

I noticed straw hats bobbing toward me. It was the Green family. Though good and kind people, they had shown the typical insensitivity of which I had already seen too much. I had overheard them talking before: "That Bud Doggy, ain't he a pitiful sight? All them airs he used to have, and look at him now." Unable to face that attitude one more time, I jumped into a ditch near the road and curled myself protectively under a plum bush.

After the Green family had passed, I still lay curled in that ditch. I sobbed wretchedly, though the tears did nothing to ease my pain. I wanted to scream out all my terror, but the hurt was too tightly locked in to roll away so easily. For an hour I lay in that ditch. I even fantasized that a rattler would come along and end my misery. None came, of course.

Eventually I crept out of my hiding place and wandered aimlessly. I passed our house. Inside were those who would give me sympathy. But the sympathy itself was a lie. I didn't want to be petted and told everything was all right. Nothing was right and it never would be. Nothing would return my arms.

I walked until I came to the A-Bye-Acre Bridge, a three-hundred-foot rainbow of steel and wood that stood fifty feet above the creek, which at that particular spot ran thirty feet deep. Often this had been my place of refuge. Today it was my last resort.

I climbed to the ledge of the bridge. Just when I started to leap, a shield-like force pressed against me and held me there. I couldn't penetrate it. I was astonished, but not afraid. I knew something extraordinary was happening.

Then I heard a voice.

"Do not throw your life away."

I looked around, but no one was in sight. Was this my imagination or had I really heard it?

The voice spoke again: *"I love you. The work you were born for still remains."*

I trembled. "What work?"

"You were born to witness the Truth, to live the Word, to bear the Miracle."

This sounded very much like the religion I had long since rejected. "I don't know nothin' about them things. And nobody's going to pay no attention to me anyhow. I'm ashamed to be seen by people, much less stand in front of them."

"Look to your right."

I gasped. Hanging in the sky were hundreds and hundreds of hands.

"What do you see?"

"I see hands without bodies floating in the sky."

"Those are my hands. They will be yours. Go now. Do the work you have been given, and doors will open before you."

My knees were now on the floor of the bridge, and tears of freedom streamed down my face as the meaning of this experience gradually sank into me. I had spoken to God and had seen His vision. He was real! My whole soul thanked and praised Him. He had felt my pain. He knew my suffering.

I had done something Bud Doggy never had—I had talked to God. I had been moved by His Spirit. No one could take that away from me.

Eleven months of midnight ended there on the bridge, ended as abruptly as they had begun. I went home rejoicing. Doors were going to swing wide for me. God had shown me the hands that were going to do it.

For a while I guarded my experience, hugging it inwardly, reluctant to share it lest others think my armlessness had driven me to see "fools' things." Though I feared the skepticism of others, the reality of what had happened deepened within me. The Bridge had been real: the armlessness was real; the pain and loneliness were real—and so were the voice and the vision. And on that day when His calming voice spoke and His vision of hands hung across the sky, the living God had become unquestionably real to me as well.

I had deceived myself for seventeen years. I had lived by pride—fragile values marked by flurries of physical accomplishment and endless activity. This deception worked until the Wire of truth burned away my defenses. Now as my self-awareness deepened, I named those defenses: guts or the willingness to tackle anything that came along; endurance; competitiveness; independence; style; and lies—such as the one I had told about getting religion. There were a lot of things about me that needed reordering.

One hot, dry day after the Bridge experience, I sat under the thick coolness of the lima bean vines on the porch of our shanty reflecting on my new life and God's purpose for it. In the course of my reflections I went to the pump for a drink of water. Working that pump continued to be one of my most difficult tasks. Gripping the handle in the crook of my knee, I pumped until the cool liquid overflowed the pail. Watching the flow, I realized that God had put the water there long before I was born, knowing that I, His son, would need it. Yet I still had to take the initiative and pump; otherwise, the water would remain in the ground. It did not matter that I had no arms. If I wanted water, I had to pump.

That metaphor spread from the pump into everything. God gave the air, but I had to breathe it. God gave me a mind, but I had to use it. God gave the ground, but I had to plant it. I had to do my own rejoicing, my own suffering. I had to keep on pumping—pumping in the faith that with His help I could do things that did not seem possible for me.

It was the most profound realization that had ever come to me. The hours moved quickly in the excitement of my discovery. Evening was beginning to trap the edges of the afternoon and the bean vines cast long shadows as I rose to greet the folks returning from the fields. I went forward to greet them eagerly, impatient to put into motion what I had learned that afternoon.

"I know now, long as I keep pumpin' and pumpin' right, I'se gonna win. And nothin', nothin' but me can stop me now. 'Cause I know who I is, why I'se here, and what I gotta do. I got faith to live by and a purpose to live for. I ain't just Bud Doggy no more. I'se a son of God, and that makes me a real somebody."

Other
Hands

EIGHT MONTHS PASSED after that shattering experience, and my circumstances remained virtually unchanged. My born-again victory had given me some inner peace, but no arms. I was still a disfigured colored boy, no more able to plow a field, saw a log, or embrace Diana than I had been before.

I realized that more than ringing declarations were required of me. Applying this faith was frighteningly difficult at times. Powerful impulses that would not stay asleep, and a guilty conscience that would not hush up, frequently returned to challenge and haunt me. At times I leaped back into my old Bud Doggy role to escape—a role I knew and still admired. But I could not stay in it for long. The guilt was too discomforting.

Then one day God reached out again and got hold of me. I guess He must have known that it was going to take more than a born-again experience to "get this nigger a-movin'."

Providentially, I discovered a place called Providence. I had never heard of this community that was situated some seven miles up the road from the Rushing shanty. My introduction to it came as the result of

Daddy's promise to Mrs. Hardy. She was an illiterate and alcoholic woman who wanted me to accompany her to the clinic in Providence so I could read her prescription for her. The idea of the trip did not excite me much, but I had no good reason not to honor Daddy's promise.

I arrived at Mrs. Hardy's shanty promptly, and within minutes she came out wheezing and staggering. As she stumbled into the front seat of the car, her drunken state saddened me enough to ask, "How is you, Miz Hardy?"

"I ain't feelin' my best, Bud Doggy," she said, steadying the jar of moonshine to her toothless mouth. "An' how is you?"

"Just fine, Miz Hardy."

"Well, when you young, you can say that, Bud Doggy."

Leavin' that moonshine alone help a-heap, too, I thought.

The ancient car, driven by her son Bob, shuddered and groaned each time it crawled a hill. I sat real still, almost breathless, fearful that I might be trapped on the road with him and the helpless woman.

Mrs. Hardy turned to me. "I ask you to come, Bud Doggy, to help me understand them doctor's orders. I don't know them big words he be usin'. I'se so glad you could come." With her trembling hand she once more lifted the moonshine to her avid lips.

"I'se very happy to help you out, Miz Hardy," I lied as my stomach lurched from the smell of alcohol mixed with dust and fumes.

Mrs. Hardy had always been warm to me. Before the accident she had told me many times how highly she regarded me. In the darkest hours after the accident she had been one of the few who made me feel like a real person. I liked her well enough to regret seeing her waste her life this way.

At the Providence Medical Clinic, we entered the area marked off by the neatly lettered sign: "For Colored Only." The sign was not unusual. Each day I lived the reality that it symbolized. We entered the waiting room. A few minutes passed. Mrs. Hardy, now bleary-eyed, began to nod, while Bob fidgeted, looking for something to do with his hands and time. I watched the other patients to relieve my own boredom. Soon a tall white woman in a nurse's uniform came over to us.

"How are you, Mrs. Hardy?" she asked, her face pleasant.

I was startled. This was the first time I had heard a white person address a colored person as "Mrs." and I wondered if it was a slip of the tongue. As the large clock on the wall slowly ticked off the minutes, I reflected on this form of address. Men and women who appeared to be about Mrs. Hardy's age were called "Aunt" and "Uncle" by the decent white folks; and the not-so-decent called them whatever came to mind. Yet the manner of the nurse seemed to be sincere.

"Dr. Minter will see you now, Mrs. Hardy."

That made it twice. It could not be a mistake.

Twenty minutes later the nurse directed me in to see Dr. Minter who repeated to me the instructions he had given Mrs. Hardy. I was flattered that this obviously educated white man should be so confident of my ability to grasp his words. When I tried to read his prescription, however, I was mystified. I simply could not make sense of it.

When our business at the clinic was finished, we went on to the Providence store. Inside, I saw a handsome ebony woman who was very much in command. The manager? The realization hit me that here in Providence I was in a different world from the one I knew seven miles down the road. Never had I been in, or even heard of, a store that was run by a colored person—and a woman at that!

"What will you have, young man?" the woman asked.

"A bar of Brock candy."

"Where would you like it?"

"Shirt pocket, ma'am. Nickel there too."

She made the exchange, smiled warmly, and said, "I'm Fannie Booker."

"I'se Bud Doggy Rushing."

"I've heard about you. What are you doing with yourself now?"

"Nothin', really."

"Have you thought about going to school?"

"Yes, ma'am, I'se been thinkin' about it a lot, but I ain't work it out yet."

"Well, we have a camp down here each summer in July. Maybe you'd like to come?"

"I—er, I think so," I hesitated, flattered by her attention and not wanting to refuse, but wondering what this "camp" was all about.

A man then interrupted us in a firm, clear voice. "Mrs. Booker, would you add a case of cheese and five pounds of six-penny nails to that order, please?"

89

"Certainly," she replied, and then added, "Mr. Cox, this is Bud Doggy, the one from the Valley."

Mr. Cox was a tall white man with a strong forehead and bushy eyebrows. I was immediately impressed by his friendliness.

"Is this your first time around here?"

"Yes, sir."

"Well, I'm glad to meet you. Come back and see us."

"Thank you, sir. I will." Though this was just conversation, I suddenly had the feeling that I would see him again.

As Mrs. Hardy and I returned to the car, Mrs. Booker came running out of the store to intercept us. "Just a minute, Bud Doggy. Here's an application form for the camp. You might want to look it over."

We shouted good-bys and left. Through the rear window I saw Mrs. Booker standing by the gas pump and waving. *Some woman!* I thought. *Some woman!*

I was so excited about my new experience that I didn't notice anything on the drive back to the plantation. I was anxious to learn about the camp, but was also fearful. Would there be a lot of strangers looking at me and asking questions? Could I handle that?

I told Momma all about my day as she chopped vegetables for supper.

It turned out that Momma knew about the place. "Bud Doggy, that place been there some time now. They run a co-op, a credit union, and a medical service. Them white folks believe in treatin' everyone the same way. They call it equality."

I showed her the application form.

"You really would like to go, huh?" she asked.

"Yes, ma'am, I think so."

"Well, I think that camp would be real good for you. I'll talk to your daddy."

Daddy signed the application form, and we began to prepare for my first trip to camp. A nervous joy filled me. I had something else to thank God for.

Nearly one hundred campers streamed into Providence, swaying under the weight of their tuition: cornmeal, fruit, beans, peas, lard, butter, salt pork, ham. Many were old friends. The new people got introduced.

The old plantation bells summoned us to orientation. All my life such bells had clanged me to action: rousting me out of bed, sending me to the field, telling me when fire or death had struck. But this was the first time they had called me to hope and dignity. Mrs. Booker explained the schedule of activities: mornings were devoted to classroom lessons, afternoons to crafts and games.

I still didn't know how the others would react to an armless classmate, but was soon reassured. The girl on my left greeted me, touching my face with her hand, and the fellow on my right gently tugged my sleeve. She was Gloria; he was Ben, her boyfriend.

We were divided into small groups and told to await our counselors. Ben was in my group, and we chatted until Reverend Coleman arrived to show us to our quarters. Ben grabbed my suitcase without being asked, and together we struck out over the carpet of lawn for the half-mile walk to the dormitory. I found it easy to accept Ben's help. In darker times my helplessness would have festered into defensiveness, but now I smiled inside and out.

"Thanks, Ben." These words also came easily now.

He grinned. "Don't mention it, man."

Ben told me he was Mrs. Booker's cousin from Chicago. For Bubba and me Chicago had seemed like Baghdad. I told Ben some of the accounts we had heard from fellows who had left the Valley and returned city-wise.

"Man," they said, "they ain't no place in the world like Chicago." They described a Promised Land where "colored folks can do anything white folks can." Some of them drove long, shiny cars and had rolls of money peeping from their pockets. Some of them even carried switchblades and guns as proof of their status.

"Don't pay no attention to that stuff, man," Ben told me firmly "Chicago ain't like that at all."

He went on to tell about the slums and crowded kitchenette apartments. When he saw how his words had disillusioned me, he quickly amended them. "Naturally, some colored people live pretty good. Got good jobs and own homes. Some even got little businesses and get elected. But honest, Bud Doggy, a lot of them have it pretty hard. A lotta those big cars you see are rented, and them white girlfriends they brag on usually are nothing but white trash."

"What's white trash?"

"Y'all call them peckerwoods down here."

Reverend Coleman came to summon us to dinner, and Ben waved me on. "I'll catch up with you."

On the way to the dining hall I stopped to examine the outdoor showers that Reverend Coleman pointed out to us. I had never seen a shower.

Ben caught up to me. "You ever used a shower?"

"Naw, man, I ain't."

"You'll like it. 'Specially when the sun is out and the water is warm. But when it come out cold . . . whoo—ee!" He gave an exaggerated shiver. We strolled on to the dining hall, linking up with Gloria on the way.

It was Gloria who helped feed me that day, the first person to hold a fork or a spoon to my mouth since the day I returned from the hospital. I peeped around to see if anyone was watching, but they were too busy eating.

Like most of the students at the camp, Gloria came from one of the communities in Holmes County where colored people had owned their own land for generations. In these rare places colored folks were isolated enough from whites that they developed more independence than those raised on plantations. Gloria's warm acceptance of me reflected the security she had always known as well as her personal friendliness.

That night as I lay on my bunk, I watched the guys roughhousing and listened to them mooning over the pretty girls.

"Man, did you see the one built like a Coke bottle and wrigglin' like a duck? I bet she is really great."

"I'm gonna get her," said another.

"Not if I beat you to her."

"Both of you gonna end up gettin' your rumps kicked outta camp if you ain't careful," said an old-timer. "Then I be gettin' them all myself."

"Lights out!" bellowed Reverend Coleman. The room quickly turned dark and quiet.

I snuggled down between the heavily starched sheets. A marvelous thing was happening to me. I could hardly wait for morning.

The next morning I sat in class, eager to learn. Once more I found myself the absolute country boy, behind in everything. The teachers were neatly dressed and spoke with clarity; they seemed to know so much. I determined to imitate everything about them—their table manners, their clothing, their speech—and began practicing when no one could see or overhear.

I was moved forward by a swirl of people and events. Mrs. Booker, who was childless, informally adopted me. She loved me, and I learned to love her. And when I wasn't reading, playing checkers, or coaching softball, I pestered any teacher who seemed to have a minute to spare. They sensed my burning desire to learn and took a personal interest in me. None of them personally knew anyone with my disability, but they all believed it was possible for me to finish school, take a job, get married, and have children. And because they believed, I believed.

One who took a personal interest in me was Reverend Coleman, the first professionally trained minister I had met. He helped me understand the importance of history and culture in relation to what the Bible said, though his style was different from any of the preachers I had known in the Valley. It took some getting used to. The man simply couldn't "whoop"—that sing-song rising to a crescendo that folks in the Valley identified with the arrival of the Spirit. Reverend Coleman also knew books. He introduced me to W. E. B. Dubois and Carter G. Woodson, the well-known black historian. Inspired by Helen Keller, George Washington Carver, Abraham Lincoln, and others who had overcome adversity, I sensed the vision of the hands becoming real. Through Gloria and Ben, Reverend Coleman, Mrs. Booker, and folks like the Coxes and the Minters, I was seeing some of those hands working in my life with great love.

Moreover, I saw that God's provision for me was somehow locked up in the white man's world. That was where the educational opportunity seemed to be. So if I was ever to succeed, I had to learn to interact with that world.

Mixed emotions warred within me as I stood in front of the Coxes' ranch house the last week of camp. There was pride—this was my first invitation to dine with a white family. And there was guilt—I had no business being in this place, as my Granddaddy Forty-Four would have been the first to tell me.

The Coxes were unlike any white people I had known. They treated colored people the same as whites. I had seen Mr. Cox hold the door for black women, and had heard that they let their children swim with the black children of the community. Perhaps they were Jew folks or abolitionist Quakers like Momma had told me about. In any case, Forty-Four would have said to let them alone.

Timidly I knocked. Mrs. Cox came to the door and welcomed me warmly.

"Dinner will be ready shortly," she said. "Would you mind waiting in the living room?" Then she hurried back to the kitchen.

Before me were the comforts of middle-class, white American life, none of which I had ever seen firsthand before. Homemade cypress-knee electric lamps glowed softly, lighting the sturdy wood furnishings and the rough, hardwood floors. Books lined the shelves like patient friends. The warm atmosphere was as real as the delicious smells streaming from the kitchen.

Yet I could hear Forty-Four talking to me as forcefully as if he were there. He kept plucking away at my conscience. "Whenever them niggers get all up in them peckerwoods' faces, they just go crazy, forget 'bout who they is. When you see a nigger doin' that, he's gonna talk his rump off to them white folks."

"Don't worry, Forty-Four," I blurted half-aloud, rising from my chair. "I ain't gonna be forgettin' who I is!"

"Did you say something, Phillip?" Mrs. Cox emerged from the kitchen, ruddy and smiling.

"Oh, no, ma'am," I hastily recovered.

I was shown into the dining room where the family had assembled and where a table gleamed with silver and crystal. Mr. Cox sat by me and helped me with dinner. No one, not even their three young daughters, seemed embarrassed by my presence or my need for assistance. And it was not because they were determined to make me comfortable. They simply seemed naturally at ease and full of positive good humor. Nevertheless, I was uncomfortable. I couldn't look at them too directly or for too long without looking away. My self-consciousness bound me.

What was taking place at the Coxes' table was a complete break of a tradition I had been bound to all my life, along with all the colored and white folks I had known. This invisible barrier overshadowed their friendliness, making me unable to accept it too quickly or too readily.

"How do you feel about that, Phillip?" Mr. Cox had asked me a question. Lost in my own thoughts, I had not heard it.

"Well, I sorta agree with you, sir," I said. Was I making a fool of myself? I looked around the table and, seeing only friendly faces, got up the courage to ask where they were from originally.

"We moved here from Texas," Mr. Cox said.

Texas! That's South! I thought.

"Did you ever live up north or in another country?" I asked, still puzzled.

"No, both our families have settled in and around Texas for generations."

"Then . . . you must be Quakers?"

"Why, no. Mrs. Cox is a Presbyterian, and I belong to the Disciples of Christ church. That makes us both Christians. Why do you ask these questions, Phillip?"

"I'se just curious, that's all."

I looked hard at Mr. Cox, earnestly bent in conversation over his half-forgotten plate; his huge square forehead furrowed with lines seemed to express genuine concern for others. He was a strange mix: rough and hard-working, yet educated and fair-minded. When he felt my questioning gaze, he started to tell me about the Mississippi soil he loved so much. He had studied it, experimented with different methods of farming it, knew which crops it loved and which it would spit back. In his view, the soil would be the salvation of the county's poor, particularly the county's one thousand land-owning black families.

"What they need to do now," he said, "is plant orchards and raise cattle, not depend so much on cotton. The way to do this, Phillip, is for colored folks to join the Providence Credit Union, and through it buy and sell in bulk."

That sure makes sense, I thought.

95

"You know, son, if the poor could get a little economic clout, they would be stimulated to live better."

It still sounded strange to hear a white man worry about black folks. I did not wholly trust him. But I was listening carefully to what he had to say. He did not focus on the white power structure, but on uplifting those pressed beneath it.

"I'm sort of a loner, Phillip. The white folks don't like what I'm trying to do for the colored folks, and the colored folks don't trust me," he said ruefully.

"Yes, sir." I squirmed uneasily.

After dinner, while we were all sitting in the living room, Mr. Cox took me to a lamplit corner. "Phillip, my wife and I, and the Bookers and the Minters, would like to form an education committee to help you evaluate your prospects—if that is agreeable to you, of course. We feel you have a fine mind, and that with the benefits of a good education, you could have a worthwhile future."

No words can express the joy and excitement I felt when Mr. Cox made that offer. Dizzy with it all, I blurted out my thanks and appreciation. Yet a part of me had sensed, even expected, all along that something wonderful was going to happen.

"Now, then, Phillip," he continued quietly, "we don't think you should go to a rehabilitation institution. They are not equipped to educate you competently, and we're afraid you might hibernate and waste away in such a place." He went on to say that in his opinion, graduating from high school and college and then going on to do some kind of graduate work would increase my ability to compete in the world of the physically able.

The doors were beginning to swing open. Now I needed the courage to walk through—the courage to keep on pumping.

After long debate, my education committee selected Saint's Industrial and Literary School, twenty-three miles from Providence. Mrs. Booker wrote to Dr. Mallory, the president of the school, but received no reply. So on the last day of camp, Mrs. Booker and I set out in her automobile to collect my opportunity in person.

No sooner had Mrs. Booker parked the car and gotten out than she was met on the sidewalk by a tall, stout, very determined mulatto woman. I knew this must be Dr. Mallory. Mrs. Booker had told me about her during our trip to the school. Dr. Mallory had built a strong reputation both locally and nationally. While still in her twenties, she had almost single-handedly raised the funds to build Saint's administration building.

I got out of the car and strained to hear what the two women were saying.

"I really think his condition would create too much difficulty for him and for the other students," Dr. Mallory said. "Too much adjustment would be required. I'm very sorry, but it just won't work."

"Dr. Mallory," Mrs. Booker persisted, "Phillip went to my camp and showed a lot of promise. He worked very hard and achieved excellent grades. He learns quickly. I've seen him adapt to everything. And he taught us some things, too."

Despite her tenacity, Mrs. Booker was no match for the presence and self-confidence of Dr. Mallory. This determined woman knew how to say no, and it soon became obvious that she was not going to change her mind.

A thoroughly disappointed Mrs. Booker returned to the car.

"I'm sorry, Phillip. The door here is closed. We'll have to look somewhere else."

Knowing how dim my future was if I returned to the Valley triggered an act of desperation. I whirled away from Mrs. Booker and blocked the walkway in front of Dr. Mallory. She stopped and looked down at me as I stood braced before her..

"What is it, young man?"

"God sent me to get educated," I said. Until that moment I had no idea what to say, but now the words came tumbling out. "And I can't leave till I done it. Gotta be an independent man, and God want you to help." In spite of my quaking insides, my voice was firm.

Dr. Mallory was obviously flabbergasted at my audacity and eyed me intently but distantly. "So this is the famous Bud Doggy I keep hearing about."

"Yes, ma'am." I jutted out my chin.

"What makes you think you're going to be an independent man?"

"God tol' me, ma'am."

"I suppose since God told you that, He told you about me, too?"

"No, ma'am, He didn't. But He did show me your hands, and He want you to use them to help me."

For a moment our eyes fixed in silence. Having heard God invoked for almost everything, Dr. Mallory was not immediately impressed. But as she attempted to answer me, she was visibly bothered by my appeal. And she was changing her mind. I could feel it come over her.

The
High Cost
of Choosing

THE WEEK BEFORE I left for Saint's, I learned the price I must pay for my education. It was on a warm August day when Diana and I were on Prince Edward Hill.

Years ago, a wealthy planter named Edward had settled on this hill. He had built a large house with massive pillars and walkways leading through the Bermuda grass to the many water-collecting cisterns on the property. He had planted groves of pear, peach, apricot, and plum trees. Because Edward had built such a grand home and surrounded it with every imaginable luxury, the spot had become known as Prince Edward Hill. Nobody could remember why the property had fallen into ruin, but the crumbled remains still overlooked the upper portion of the Mississippi Delta and the Valley. And the orchards as well as an abundance of wild grapes, huckleberries, and blackberries still bore sweet, delicious fruit.

Older folks seldom went to the hill because of the mile-long climb up a washed-out road, but I loved the place and went there often. In spring and summer, the hilltop was enclosed with foliage and sweet blossoms. In autumn and winter, with the leaves gone, the view stretched out astonishingly for miles and miles to a distant horizon. As far as I was concerned, the hill was a fantastic place for playing and exploring, for thinking and dreaming.

Bubba and I had once built a skateboard from scrap wood and zoomed down the hill at terrifying speed. We'd pitched rocks into the depths of the cisterns and eaten freely of whatever fruit was in season. When our talking, playing, and eating were done, we'd lay in the shade of the old magnolia tree which seemed like the sweetest place in the world to be.

After Bubba was gone, Diana and I had begun coming here to walk and talk or just be together. On this occasion, we took our time walking up the hill as I tried to communicate my excitement at being accepted at Saint's School. I described in detail my schedule, including the math, history, science, agriculture, and English literature I would be studying. I told her stories about the white people in Providence, about the Coxes and the Minters, about Mrs. Booker, and all they had done for me. I explained that I would probably be away at school for eight or nine years and would eventually get my master's degree. Diana listened carefully and nodded her head occasionally.

When we reached the top of the highest ridge and stood looking down at the countryside, I felt we were king and queen on our own royal hill. We strolled about the ruins for awhile, then sat down in the shade of the old magnolia.

"You know, Bud Doggy, I been thinkin'," Diana's voice was soft, almost faded.

"Yes, baby?"

"Well, I just been wonderin' 'bout you goin' off to school. I wonder what it gonna be like. I mean, where we is concerned."

"I don't know exactly," I stalled.

"I love you, Bud Doggy," Diana said. "I love you plenty."

I knew Diana cared for me in ways no other woman did. Yet I didn't want her to say it. Somehow I knew talk was going to mess up our relationship. I was sure of it, and felt guilty and selfish.

"Do you really love me, Bud Doggy?"

"Sure do, baby. Don't think I can love nobody else like I love you. I still be lovin' you, no matter where I be."

"Eight or nine years, that an awful long time. Why, I be almost thirty-two years old before you get out."

She was right. It was a powerful long time, almost more than I could imagine at that age. But what alternatives did I have?

After a period of silence, Diana began to talk, almost nervously, about the money I was to get as compensation from the power and light company. Why didn't I take some of it and buy land to raise cows and other stock? Perhaps I could rent some of it out and use the income to hire help with the cows and crops.

"What you think about that, Bud Doggy?" she asked.

"It wouldn't work out," I said. "The Lawd has already showed me what I hafta do if I'se to be blessed."

Silence. Then, "Suppose you and the Lawd get together and decide on you doin' somethin' that don't include me?"

I lifted my head to see if she was joking. Her wide eyes gazed steadily into mine, meeting me head-on with everything that was unsaid between us. I had no place to hide.

"What makes you ask a question like that, Diana? God love you just like He do me."

"'Cause I really wanna know, Bud Doggy."

"The Lawd and me don't go 'round teamin' up against you, Diana."

"Ain't that what happen' on the bridge? I wasn't included then, was I?"

"I don't think you outta be sayin' things like that."

But she wouldn't drop the subject.

"I care more 'bout you than you might know, and I ain't bein' disrespectful to God. But I'se a woman now. Got womanly needs. When do I start livin'? All the time you was in the hospital, I almost went crazy . . . didn't hardly do nothin' but pray and cry 'cause I knowed you hurt so much. Everybody at home thought I was sick, but it was only thinkin' 'bout you made me that way, Bud Doggy. Since you come back, seem like I love you more. But ever since you come off that bridge you ain't the same. You is all wrapped up in books, boardin' school, and witnessin'. I wanna do more than that. I'se twenty-three years old, and I can't wait so long now."

But I was still blind and stupid. All I could think of was that my

CARL A. RUDISILL LIBRARY
LENOIR RHYNE COLLEGE

redhead was jealous! A Bud-Doggy kiss would bring her around. I pressed my lips gently to hers. As she stiffened and withdrew, I began to understand just how serious she was.

I got up and moved to a concrete block some feet away. She propped herself against the trunk of the old tree, arms wrapped around her slender legs, chin resting on her knees. Heavy silence hung between us.

I remembered the ways Diana had shown her love to me in the past. How she had come to the hospital faithfully. How she had accepted me when things seemed the worst. I loved her, too, but the marriage, land, and cow stuff was not what I needed. I didn't know for sure what I was going to do, but I had to keep myself free to find out.

Diana was ready to start her life. I still had to prepare for mine. Apparently Momma was right about age counting so much. The woman in Diana was already grown and wasn't going to wait for the man in me to grow up. She was forcing me to choose between a life with her and a dream I still didn't understand too well.

But what if I did marry her? Then I'd have a wife I loved and that might turn out very well for me, too. Diana and I had known each other for nearly ten years. She understood me and everything about me— where my skin was burnt and where they had cut off my arms. She had loved me before, during, and after the Wire. She was the one who had given me secret kisses in that hospital bed despite the stench of burned flesh. She was the one who had stayed at home with me many Saturday nights after I returned from the hospital, when she could have been out dancing and having a good time. She would sit for hours with me on her porch, talking and listening to the Grand Ole Opry or the rhythm and blues from station WDIA. We would talk about life in the Valley, how we felt about each other, how my momma thought Diana was too old for me, how both our mommas thought we were getting too serious, and how someday we might get married. It was during those days that I realized that Diana's love and respect for me were real and that our relationship was a very important thing in my life.

Now, what if this education thing wasn't God's purpose. Suppose I let her get away and then found out no woman wanted me. Would God call me foolish for letting the prettiest girl in the Valley get away from me? But if I did marry her, I'd have to give up the school.

Either way, I had to give up something. Love had a price and so did the Lord's promises. I had to choose. And I had to lose as well. Still, to exchange purpose for marriage would make Diana my future, my life, my God. No, that would not do. I would be killing the man in me for the woman in her. With no man left in me, I could never please the woman in her. And though I was too young to see or understand it at the time, we would have grown to hate ourselves and each other.

Diana's hand on my shoulder brought me back from my thoughts.

"Diana, there is a lotta ins and outs about the bridge and the school and us that I still don't understand too clear. There's so much I still gotta work out. Seem you done put out choices to me I didn't know I had.

"I been thinkin' about choices. I had to make a choice about God's way on the bridge. Now I gotta make a choice 'bout you and the school.

"Two things I know for sure, though. First, God's hand is on me good—and I'se gonna accept His way for my life. I don't know what that mean right now, where it all gonna lead and what all I gotta be doin'. But I believe that goin' off to school got a powerful lot to do with it. And the second thing is—I know I love you, Diana . . . love you very, very much."

"I know you do, Bud Doggy," she responded, putting her arms around me.

As we walked down Prince Edward Hill, I felt a strong sense of loss. Things would never be the same with Diana and me again. But I had to preserve my right to choose, no matter what the outcome.

Saint's

ON THE SUNDAY afternoon I left for Saint's, the sun shone down generously, quickening the life beneath. The Valley surged and pulsated with
gratitude. Sunflowers bowed reverently, and the golden brown of the
ripened crops reflected all the favors of the summer. The proud, young
rooster stretched and preened and made love to all the hens; the mule
nuzzled and nipped, unaware of the dirty trick the vets had performed
on him years before. Cows plodded widelegged toward home, bags
heavy with milk, and lard-fat hogs grunted their hoggishness and wal-
lowed in holes. Moles, groundhogs, and rats rooted devastatingly
through peanut and potato patches, while rabbits skipped softly through
gardens, nibbling a path from plant to plant.

Lovely young girls waited anxiously, eyeing the road. The boyfriend was on his way. He had stopped at the nearby spring to wash dust
from his face and to kill a few minutes of sunlight. He was timing his
arrival so that it would be dark enough for the elders to have left the
porch, but still light enough for his girl to see how sharp he looked,
swaggering toward her with his long coat hanging almost to his knees,

his balloon-hipped pants fitting snugly around waist and ankles. There had to be enough light so she could catch the glint of his long watch chain, admire the flowers in his wide tie and the feathers in his tub-rimmed hat, and see her reflection in his pointed shoes, hastily polished against the back of his pants moments before.

Though I was leaving home to make one of the most important journeys of my life, a good part of my thoughts were on the immediate. I was still a handicapped country boy. And I was leaving behind the caring tenderness of my family, my friends, and my girl—everything that had ever sustained me.

Daddy wriggled my last piece of luggage into the trunk of Mr. Doug's old car. My brothers and sisters clustered near the gate, while Momma looked on from the door, smoothing her apron with nervous strokes. After the other good-bys were said, I turned to her.

"Now don't forgit the Lawd, son. He makin' all this possible. You keep doin' right and He keep sending the blessings," she admonished.

"Yes, ma'am," I said as I cradled my head to her love and warmth one last time, then scooted into the car.

At Saint's School, students poured from taxicabs, from long, out-of-state cars, and from beat-up local trucks. Suitcases, footlockers, and trunks were everywhere. Mr. Doug weaved his car through the bustling campus to the men's dormitory, a long, white, frame building on a hill where I was assigned a room. These simple, functional surroundings—a bed, a chest, a chair, a desk—would be my home for the next two years.

I was the first person from a Mississippi plantation to attend Saint's. Academically, socially, and culturally, a gulf separated me from the other young men and women at the school.

Though eighteen, I was only in the ninth grade and thus was four years older than my classmates. Then there was the way I dressed: my clothes were neat but odd. And precious little money jingled in my pockets.

I studied the matter and determined to urbanize my wardrobe. I walked to town, and with six of the eleven dollars I had earned selling the *Grit,* a weekly newspaper, I purchased some clothes on layaway.

Four of the remaining dollars were spent on a bushel of peanuts, one hundred small paper bags, and cab fare back to campus. Now all I needed was permission to sell peanuts to the students.

I solved the problem by bluffing the dietician, a stout sapphire who daily stood in the dining hall, shimmering with kitchen sweat and scowling constraint. She was singularly determined to repress ghetto and country table behavior in favor of white, middle-class etiquette.

I passionately resented her lording it over us and every plateful we ate. I guess she reminded me too much of the Man's presence I wanted to leave behind. Perhaps this resentment helped ease me over my conscience as I exploited her extreme devotion to Dr. Mallory, whose every whim she indulged with the intensity of plantation Uncle Tomism. The mere words "Dr. Mallory" would robotize her. So I played on her weakness. I eyeballed her with confidence and told her what I wanted, calculating my words to imply that my project was "authorized" by Dr. Mallory. Of course, my peanuts got cooked in her kitchen.

I still had the problem of bagging them. Then a student named Charles walked into my room, asking to borrow my radio. Since he and his roommate had money, I wondered why they didn't buy their own radio, but decided to turn this to my advantage. After much haggling, I negotiated a rental fee of one dollar a week. Fifty cents of that went to hire another student to bag the peanuts for me.

From my profits selling the peanuts, I faithfully took all but ten percent to the store each Saturday to pay on my layaway. Mr. Flowers, the proprietor, just as faithfully kept track of my payments, no matter how small.

One Saturday when I entered the store, there was a large package on the counter with my name on it. And Mr. Flowers surprised me by saying, "You're an unusual boy with a lot of spunk, Phillip. I'm astonished by the effort you've made. From what I've seen, I know you'll be an excellent student. By the way, this package belongs to you. Your clothes have been paid for, so go and enjoy them." I had paid thirty-three dollars and he had paid the remaining balance on the sixty-dollar total.

More important than clothing, however, were other differences separating me from my fellow students. Many of them were very casual about education; they had come to Saint's only because their parents wanted them to be educated. For them, it was a social playground. I

106

knew I couldn't afford to be casual about my education. Success was my only alternative.

The other students seemed to find it easier to deal with my armlessness than with my other differences. Like my thick plantation dialect, spiced heavily with country idioms. I'd say things like "dat dere problem" and "de spanx of Egypt." "Dallas, Texas" came out "Dollar, Texas," and "a Kool-Aid" became something like "a cold egg." While some found me fascinating and funny, often I simply was not understood.

Though I could tolerate jokes at my expense, my speech was a clear indication of how far I had to go to catch up. Whatever the personal sacrifice, I was determined to make it. But there were questions: Could I really catch up? How long would it take? And perhaps most crucial, would an education really make a difference to a man without arms?

Another difference was caused by something I had struggled with back in the Valley: the opposite sex. Girls!

Though the school's puritanical rules added a veneer of southern-belle respectability, none of us southern boys had ever seen anything quite like the sophisticated young women from the urban north who came to Saint's. Even the most devout young men were influenced by their shapely legs and beautiful complexions, ranging from golden tan to burnished mahogany. Furthermore, these beauties lacked the untouchable innocence of the country girls; their boldness both shocked and delighted us.

Dr. Mallory must have often been hard-pressed to keep Saint's promise to parents: "If you send us an unmarried daughter, we will not send you back an unmarried mother." Nevertheless, the boys missed no opportunity to exploit the girls, whether in imagination or reality.

I was so grateful for the opportunity to attend Saint's that I wasn't about to violate Dr. Mallory's rules. Besides, to involve myself in such behavior was morally wrong. My physical disfigurement was imperfection enough; moral and academic superiority were my compensating techniques. This attitude did not make me popular. I overheard myself referred to as "Mr. Chaperone, always trying to be Mr. Good Stuff. That dude can't get his and won't let nobody else get theirs." Nevertheless, exercising such control gave me a feeling of power, and I sometimes gloated over my ability to "put the screws" to the fellows. So I persisted in my moral claims, unaware that the basis for it all was self-interest. Later, when head-on confrontations with honesty exposed by hypocrisy, I was nearly devastated.

Since getting to the girls consumed an incredible amount of energy, it was only natural that there would be nightly bull sessions in the dorm when the older, more experienced fellows made it their duty to set "the young turkeys" straight. At first I tried to ignore the convivial laughter. These sessions contradicted Dr. Mallory's teachings and the school's principles. They must be a pothole on the path to my own spirituality. But the ringleaders were good talkers with vivid descriptions of city life and its tall buildings, street gangs, skid rows, drug addicts, and prostitutes. Choice phrases filtered through.

Finally, one night, the temptation was just too strong. I shoved back my chair and joined the gang just as George started discussing prostitution. He walked about the room gesticulating like a professor expounding a profound topic.

"Do they really sell sex, man?" asked Mac, the eighteen-year-old son of a Mississippi preacher.

"Durn right they do."

"How much they charge?"

"All depends whether she's low or high class," George explained. "The low class one is really hard up and a hard looker too. Needs lotsa makeup. Usually hooked on somethin'. Begs for buyers for as low as two bucks a trip. Now, the high class ones wear expensive rags, furs, and jewels. Look real good, too. They won't hardly turn loose for less than ten bucks."

"A nigger gotta be stoned crazy to give up that much dough for somethin' like that," someone commented, and laughter rocked the room.

"Niggers ain't the only ones, man," interjected Bill, a senior from Detroit, Michigan. "White folks are doin' it too." Again everyone laughed.

I rebuked myself for spending time in this way, and with that resolve tried to introduce a more serious level of discussion into the nightly sessions. For one thing, I shared with them experiences I knew about—conditions on the Mississippi Delta plantations. I told of men chained in gangs, covered with dust, clanking miserably past our door, and of the heartaches of the poor. And I told my own story of how the Wire had killed Bubba and nearly taken me.

Amazingly, I discovered that I could be myself and still be accepted. My confidence increased. As that happened, I found that I could be more sensitive to the needs of others and more accepting of them. By attempting to help others see God's love and power, I found more love for myself.

"You always so together, man, like nothin' bothers you," they often said. These comments touched me deeply. I remembered a time I had not been together at all, a time—not all that long ago—when I had been too ashamed even to be seen, much less call attention to myself.

Although I was gaining the respect of my fellow students and even a measure of self-respect, I still had to battle daily with incompassionate desks, bookshelves, and pencil sharpeners. Though teachers and students did their best to help, the world of inanimate objects perversely set out a host of little obstacles. I didn't always have the privacy to work on them as I had back home, but I was determined not to be beaten by doorknobs and chalkboards. Small accomplishments once more became major victories.

I opened doors by slipping off my shoes and turning the doorknobs with my feet. When I finally hit upon the idea of having holes cut in my socks to give me more gripping power on the slippery knobs, the technique was perfected.

Chairs with built-in desks for righthanded students were awkward enough for the lefthanded, but nearly impossible for one who wrote with his mouth. However, by sitting sideways in one and using another for a table, I managed well.

At first some girls offered to share their notes with me, but they ended up borrowing mine when they found that mine were more complete. Pencils, however, were made to comply with yielding fingers, not with the cutting edge of teeth. Pressure frequently popped them in two, until pencil pieces heaped around me like scattered cigarette butts. But I preferred them to leaky ballpoint pens that spit inky blobs on my paper. I remedied the snapping by having pencils fortified with layers of rubber bands. The spitting pens I had to live with.

My blackboard assignments were done on a piece of paper which the teacher or another student could fasten to the board. I asked instructors to call on me in class, reminding them that I could not raise my hand to volunteer. Thus, one by one the problems dropped away and others took their place.

But I did all my own themes and papers, took my own tests, and usually finished first or second in my class. I made the honor roll and dean's list every semester, and only one student had a higher average than mine. That I could finish early and make better grades than most fired my competitive spirit and rekindled my arrogance. This zealousness spawned jealousy of those whose marks rivaled or surpassed mine. In a way, my old Bud-Doggy self crept back.

In my secret resentment, I became dishonest with students who thought I was what I said I was—a reborn son of God. I became reluctant to share my notes or even contribute what I knew in joint study sessions. I was tempted to allow or participate in gossip when it concerned top students. Though others looked up to me because they believed I had a faith that enabled me to give up things they were not willing to surrender, I knew I was a hypocrite. Searching for an answer to my predicament, I read the Bible and prayed almost feverishly. And I learned that being born again did not make one instantly perfect. I had to practice my faith on a regular, daily basis. That kind of commitment was a lot tougher than being Bud Doggy.

Days
of
Promise

DURING THAT FIRST year at Saint's, two days stood out as especially noteworthy, as landmarks of promise and hope. The first was Pilgrim's Day, and I learned about it on a beautiful November afternoon as I strolled across the campus toward the library. Though drinking in the warm reds and golds of autumn, I could not help but notice the unusual activity going on all about me. Students and faculty alike seemed preoccupied with picking up loose sticks and branches, raking leaves, pruning shrubbery, sweeping sidewalks, and mending steps and fences. While outside, fence posts, gates, and tree trunks were being whitewashed, inside floors were buffed until they were slippery.

I asked a passing senior what was happening. He pointed to a poster advertising something called Pilgrim's Day. "It's an annual day when people come from all over the country to visit the school. We call 'em pilgrims."

"Who is these pilgrim folks?"

"Preachers, bishops, overseers, church mothers, elders . . . anybody who supports the school."

"Are they colored folks?"

111

"Why, yes."

"You sho? I mean, is they all colored?"

"Yes," he replied again, obviously puzzled by my question.

I continued on my way to the library, thinking about what I had just heard and wondering what these bishops and church mothers would look like. All the preparation puzzled me, too; I had never known colored folks to go to such extremes to honor other colored folks. To be honored, people must be grand and important, and I could not imagine any colored folks being that grand or important.

The next day, limousines and chartered buses filed through the campus disgorging hundreds. They wore mink, Stetson hats, Stacy Adams shoes, and mohair suits. Despite their finery, no makeup caked their faces; no cigarette stains colored their fingers; no snuff browned their teeth and gums; no alcohol polluted their breath. I could not believe what I was seeing.

But the reason I remembered those pilgrims long after they left had nothing to do with their fine clothes or big cars or sweet-smelling appearance. I remembered them because they knew who I was. Dr. Mallory must have told them about my situation. As a result, they reached out to me with genuine caring in their eyes, in their voices, and in their touch. They praised my determination and urged me to call on them for anything I needed. Later, many sent me money, clothing, and letters of encouragement. I was a person to them. I was not invisible.

Though I still had not seen an armless black man, let alone an educated armless black man, I was seeing educated black men and women. And there had to be a first time for the armless one. *Perhaps that first one would be me.*

The other landmark that year was May Day. Throughout the school year, students of all twelve classes raised funds for the school. The boy and girl who raised the most money were then crowned king and queen for May Day. That year I raised eight hundred dollars, mostly from the sale of peanuts and garden seeds, and was awarded the honor of being the king.

For an entire week before May Day, the staff and students were our loyal servants, bowing and curtseying, carrying books, and obeying any reasonable command—making us feel like royalty. In the cafeteria, we ate at a lace-covered table and were served on fine china and heavy silverware.

During this week, I took my first airplane ride when the queen and I were flown from Jackson to New Orleans to be fitted for royal robes.

As we boarded the Delta DC-3, I looked for the colored section, but found none. I felt as though I shouldn't sit just anywhere, but finally took a window seat.

"Don't they have separate sections for colored?" I asked Mrs. Powell, our chaperone.

"No, Bud Doggy," she replied in a low tone. "Not in airplanes."

At cruising altitude, strong currents bounced the plane about rather roughly. As my ears clogged and nausea threatened, I remembered how Daddy and I used to watch crop-dusters spray for boll weevils. Once we saw one nearly crash into a clump of trees. "I ain't never gonna ride in no plane with no white man drivin' it," Daddy told me. "'Cause if somethin' go wrong, he gonna be tellin' me to get out on the wing and check it out."

We hit another air pocket and my sickness got worse. The stewardess detected my discomfort and asked if I needed anything.

"No, ma'am," I said, too proud to admit my difficulty. She smiled and produced a paper bag which she put on the ledge beside me.

By now my insides felt like they wanted to come out every way they could, but I was terrified at the prospect of making a fuss. Besides, I wasn't sure whether I needed to vomit into the bag or sit on it!

Fortunately, we landed before I had to decide.

My stomach settled back to normal in the cab that took us to downtown New Orleans. We were taken to a huge, white, antebellum house, and Mrs. Powell registered us in a lobby resplendent with ornate high ceilings and magnificent chandeliers. The proprietor of this hotel for colored folks was a strikingly handsome brown-skinned woman with an accent I first took to be African. Later Mrs. Powell told me she was a Creole.

We were ushered up a great staircase with dark banisters and thick carpeting. In our rooms, Mrs. Powell pointed out that the pictures on the wall were real oil paintings and that the furniture was antique, but the words "antique" and "paintings on canvas" didn't mean much to me. I was content just to listen and absorb myself in the intricate wood patterns of the high-backed beds and the warm colors of the bedspreads.

That afternoon the queen and I were measured for our blue and white coronation costumes, complete with capes and crowns. This was followed by a real New Orleans dinner featuring gumbo soup. Dr. Mallory had prepared us for this famous Louisiana dish with mouth-watering descriptions. "Make sure the king and queen get some gumbo," had been her parting words to Mrs. Powell at the airport. But the spicy soup seemed less delicious than Momma's Valley succotash.

The next day, while the others slept, I eased from the hotel into the brisk New Orleans morning. The desire to walk alone had been nudging away in me. Since leaving the school I had been surrounded by people—at the airport, on the plane, and at the hotel. I was desperate to be alone.

This was the first real city I had ever seen, and I wanted to see as much as I could. So I ventured further and further from the hotel, allowing myself to be caught up in the traffic noises and the shop windows and the general excitement of the city. All those people, cars, buses, and buildings were a new dimension for a country boy. White folks, colored folks, short folks, tall folks, all kinds of folks poured along the sidewalk. But I was still the only one without arms.

Pressing armless against the human traffic sometimes caused me to come close to losing my balance. But even then people did not seem to notice me. In fact, they did not seem to see or hear. It was as though they were robots, their destination set, oblivious to everything else. No one stared at my empty sleeves. They didn't care enough to stare.

I walked for about an hour, then decided I should return to the hotel so Mrs. Powell wouldn't be worried. As I tried to retrace my route, nothing looked familiar. After a few blocks, anxiety hammered within me. I stopped dead in my tracks. I was lost. For all the Bud-Doggy independence I always bragged about and prided myself on, I leaned a good deal on others. And I had a lot less confidence than others when it came to new situations.

Finally I got a traffic officer's attention. "Sir, I'm lost. Can you tell me how to get to the hotel?"

"Which hotel you lookin' for, boy?"

114

"The Creole-lady hotel, sir." My mind was blank. I couldn't remember the name.

He eyed me skeptically. "Never heard of it. What's the address?"

"I . . . I don't know."

"Sorry, boy, can't help you." The officer resumed doing what he knew best: directing humans who knew where they were going, but who, because they didn't see each other, had to be kept out of each other's way.

A cabby finally helped me find my way back to the hotel—and nobody had to look far to find me for the rest of the trip. But, though there were spaces out there beyond my measure, I had taken a look and knew they were conquerable.

On May Day, in heat that threatened to crack even royal composure, the parade got under way. The honor guard stepped forward smartly. Majorettes followed, swinging into their drill with precision. Hundreds of spectators perched on the edges of rooftops, astride tree branches, or atop vehicles. They had come from all over the district by car, wagon, horse, and mule. From the royal float all I could see was a sea of smiling faces, colored and white. Hands waved red-white-and-blue flags and everyone shouted, "God save the king and queen."

At one point I saw my family standing in the midst of the crowd, straining to get a good look at me. Their faces were filled with loving pride. I smiled as I had never smiled before. Then I froze. Diana was with them! Why was she here? Did she still think of me? Did she miss me the way I missed her? The queen must have noticed my distraction, for she elbowed me gently. I sat up straight, then tilted my head with dignity to our subjects.

Back on the campus after the parade, every athletic feat imaginable was performed in our honor. I drank in the entire scene: white men with their ladies; mothers and fathers glowing with pride; bent-over grandfathers cheering their grandchildren to the finish line; middle-aged church women mingling with bronzed young athletes. May Day was a success.

Tomorrow the robes would go back to New Orleans and the athletic gear would be stowed away. Merchants who had shoveled in the benefits would throw out the debris. Folks would return to the hills, swamps, and hollows, once again loyal subjects of plantation chores. Ropes and banners would come down, and the police would go back to being The Man in the street.

Tomorrow I would go back to being Bud Doggy. But the fleeting moments of simulated royalty had enduring benefits. Somehow, they were concrete proof that the well of life rewards at some time in some measure, be it small or great, the one who goes on pumping, no matter who he is.

May Day seemed a reaffirmation that I existed in God's blessing.

My Words . . .
His Word

SAINT'S SCHOOL GAVE me much more than a formal education. It took me a long way from the Valley and from that initial encounter with Dr. Mallory on the walk. Yet the further I traveled, the more I understood that success and power were in The Man's ubiquitous hands; he was in charge—reaching, possessing, and always getting more. While I, left with the trappings of plantation ignorance, had little power to snatch my blessing from those hands.

Nothing symbolized that ignorance, that powerlessness, more than my dialect.

"Words have power, Phillip. You must learn to use them effectively," Dr. Mallory said. "Lincoln and Churchill used words to help save their countries. Douglass used them to help free his people, Washington to build a school for them." Dr. Mallory herself was an accomplished speaker whose distinct syllables suffered no dropped suffix or prefix. Her oratory dug hundred dollar bills from the pockets of colored people I thought were flat broke, and thousand dollar checks from white Mississippians I thought were completely indifferent to the problems of blacks. I determined to speak like her.

With both patience and merciless drill she taught me. She gave me material to recite and sat unyieldingly in the back of the empty auditorium while I struggled on the stage to gesture with my body and to punctuate my voice. In time I progressed through practice sentences to a reasonable version of well-known prose and poetry.

This wasn't just altruism on her part. Unashamedly opportunistic when it came to Saint's, and always on the lookout for ways to raise money, Dr. Mallory saw in my handicap an effective public relations device. She incorporated my oratorical success into the school's frequent fund-raising activities, sending me on the road with the glee club and the band. Later I would see this as a compromise of my personal dignity that would bring me into unbearable conflict with her. But though some of Dr. Mallory's motives may have been questionable, the long-term benefits were immeasurable.

I can mark these benefits to me from my very first fund-raising venture, when a group of us attended the National Convocation of the Church of God in Christ in Memphis, Tennessee. About five thousand church members from all parts of the country filled the Mason Temple each day. Many had scrimped and saved all year for this event. Here they forgot problems and disappointments. Here there were no snooping welfare workers, no repossessed cars, no eviction notices, no bill collectors, and no demeaning social system. The bond of brotherhood made them one, unifying doctors, teachers, businessmen, garbage collectors, welfare recipients, and illiterates. All had their "somebodyness" affirmed and their faith validated in a way unique to this place.

One night was designated Saint's School Night. Just before the service, those of us scheduled to perform met with Dr. Mallory for final instructions and prayer. She told us to do our best and then marched us to the pulpit.

Along the walls of the huge temple were abandoned wheelchairs, braces, and crutches left in testimony to the healing power of the merciful God. As I sat in the front, my eyes returned again and again to those joyless instruments. Without warning, my own desire to be healed rose from the depths of my subconscious—a desire that had lain quivering inside, successfully repressed it had seemed, never until now expressed.

"Lord, give me back my arms!" I blurted.

I had not asked for my arms since the bridge experience, though I had attended charismatic services and had heard people testify that they had been healed. After my rebirth, I felt it was God's will that my arms not be restored. Now the evidence lining the walls renewed my hope for a miracle.

If ever I'm to be healed, now is the time and place, I thought. *Maybe that's why the Lord brought me to this place, so He can heal me in the presence of all these witnesses. That really would be something. . . .*

A thudding murmur redirected my thoughts. The crowd now stood, their eyes gazing as one upon the frail little man who stepped to the pulpit: Bishop Charles Harrison Mason. I had never seen him before, but had heard a great deal about him. "He's saintly . . . a genius . . . preacher, teacher, and healer," both teachers and students said. His presence fired my hopes even more.

The knots of excitement tightened as my turn came to speak. I must have done well, for the audience responded with hearty applause. The knots intensified as the slight figure rose and made his way toward me after I finished. I was almost faint with expectation as Bishop Mason first complimented me and then placed his trembling, wizened hands on my head and anointed me with prayer. I shut my eyes and closed out the world—inside it was only God and me. Then I prayed, too.

"O Lord, my God, you know I love you, and you know I accept your will. But please, O Lord, hear the cry of your child tonight and give me back my arms. You know I've been hurt so deeply and suffered so much because I don't have my arms. I'm tired of hurting, Lord, tired of suffering, tired of being dependent on other folks' hands. Please, dear God, give them back to me!"

Could God heal me? Yes, He could do anything He wanted to do. My sleeves were going to be filled the way they were before the Wire. I was going to feel the ballooning of my flesh against the cloth. I had never before prayed so deeply. If the return of my arms was possible, it would happen on this platform.

Blind and deaf to the audience and the bishop, I didn't hear his "amen" or feel him lift his hands from me. I didn't know he sat down while I still stood praying with my whole soul, pleading for God to grant what He had withheld in the past.

Finally I ended my prayer, frozen to the floor behind the pulpit, afraid to open my eyes. I heard no shouts, no cries of joy.

My emotions stirred like rats: ugly wriggling doubt, disappointment, shame, and bitterness.

My arms had not returned.

I was hardly conscious of what happened after that, though I knew Bishop Mason asked the crowd to bless me, and I could hear the people singing as the plate went around. I stood to accept the generous offering of almost four thousand dollars, grateful and glad for the school, but numb for myself.

How would I escape the consequences of my prayer? What did this mean for my faith? Why had God failed me?

Is this God's final answer? I agonized. *Perhaps . . . perhaps by not giving me my miracle He is showing me that I must be strong. Perhaps He is saying that my strength isn't in my arms, but in accepting His plan for my life. Maybe He hasn't failed me after all. Maybe He has blessed me.*

Hope died hard. But as these thoughts came to me—through His Spirit I know—my tensely hunched shoulders straightened and relaxed. I didn't know whether I would ever let my hope of a miracle go completely, but that night, in that place, I vowed I would never again anguish over my armlessness.

"From now on, O Lord," I prayed, "help me to rejoice in what I have, and help me, dear Jesus, not to weep over what I don't have."

I resolved to accept my condition as the will of God and to live a productive life in spite of it.

That night I, too, left a witness, albeit invisible, of a healing miracle. Left with the discarded wheelchairs, crutches, and braces were my surrendered hopes of having my arms restored—a testimony to a God who could not be compelled or coaxed, a God who could not be prayed into doing my pumping for me, a God who knew the best plan for my life.

Temptation

THERE WAS ANOTHER trapping I carried with me from the Valley that threatened to snatch God's blessing from me, and it was much more difficult to eradicate than a dialect, much harder to educate than the mind. This was my view of sex and my own physical needs.

This became evident to me one night when my speaking activities took me to the city of St. Louis. An hour or more before the performance, I strolled out for a walk and promptly found myself in the red-light district. Since those nightly bull sessions at school I had been curious to see this aspect of city life for myself. And here it was: painted women hiding tired eyes behind caked mascara, flickering neon signs, loud derisive music, well-dressed pimps (dudes) with women hanging on their arms like grapes on a vine. The Man was there, too, strutting the beat, his nightstick and flaunted power ready to take on any colored who decided to go crazy and think he, and not The Man, was boss of the street.

I walked around, taking it all in and forgetting all about the time. When I remembered Dr. Mallory and my speaking engagement, I retraced my steps in a panic. I ducked into the side entrance of the church just as she was introducing me.

"Now we have a remarkable young man, brought up from the mud of Mississippi. I am pleased to present—Phillip Rushing."

I tried not to betray the butterflies in my stomach by holding my head high and walking quickly and purposefully to the lectern.

"I will now recite 'For My People,' a poem by Margaret Walker," I began. In accordance with the mannerisms I had been taught, I stepped backward, bowed my head, closed my eyes, raised my head again, and sounded off.

The first half went fine. Then I blanked out completely! I couldn't remember the rest of Walker's poem! But I knew better than to stop talking. Taking great care not to look at Dr. Mallory, I began to ad-lib, improvising from my own experiences, turning them into a solemn composition much like the forgotten poem.

When I finished, the audience gave me a standing ovation. Dr. Mallory had taught me well; I knew how to please them on my own.

Afterward, Dr. Mallory pulled me aside. "Phillip, you forgot your poem tonight. However, I must compliment you on the way you worked out of it. From now on, keep your mind on what you are doing. It's dishonest to tell them you are going to recite an author's work and then do something else."

Later, in my room, I searched out the reason for my forgetfulness. Why had I forgotten that poem? Did it have anything to do with my visit to the red-light district? What was I doing there at all? How could I stand before others and accept their praise when I had just been visiting a place like that? The dishonesty I saw within myself seemed much worse than my dishonesty about the poem.

I was torn by fear and temptation, for I knew my visit to the red-light district was hardly an accident. It was a symptom of my repressed sexual attitudes and needs. For years I had tried to ignore these attitudes and needs; now they were surfacing. Perhaps the Lord wanted to deal with them as He had with my pride and hypocrisy in other areas of my life.

My sexual attitudes were a hodgepodge of Valley fundamentalism, my perception of the "morally good life," and personal fears concerning my own sexuality.

The Valley folks held premarital and extramarital sex to be wrong on biblical authority and backed their views with chapter and verse. At the same time, however, they grossly contradicted themselves with myths and social attitudes that praised sexual performance. So in reality, mothers' fears and husbands' insecurities, not fidelity to the Scriptures, perpetuated these views.

The ability to dominate was the most important male consideration and marked the "sho-nuff man." Good looks were important, but not nearly as important as domination. "How you look make it possible to get her attention, but how you love her gonna determine if you keep her." Losing your wife to another man was irrefutable proof that you lacked "bed power" and were something less than a "sho-nuff man." Men who had been victims of this belief—and there were many in the Valley—went around with their heads ducked in shame. In self-defense, therefore, husbands invoked the biblical prohibitions to control their wives, even if they ignored the other teachings of Scripture. "The Lawd got sharp eyes and can see you messin' 'round even when I can't," the men would often say.

All this created a vicious circle, of course. To prove they were "sho-nuff men," the men had to attract and dominate women. Furthermore, men who were reluctant to "sow their wild oats," or who "sowed" infrequently, were labeled "sissies," a term so shameful that some became promiscuous just to escape it. And that often meant attracting and dominating another man's wife. So, faithfulness was relative. What was good for the goose was definitely not good for the gander.

While husbands did not believe the sexual commandments applied equally to them, the wives seemed confident that the commandments were intended mainly for teen-age daughters. But daughters had nothing but contrary examples in both Daddy *and* Momma.

However, there was one clear principle of honor: if you made a girl pregnant, you were expected to marry her. Anything less was an outrage, for it brought shame to the girl's family and made her an object of abuse. If a girl could not snare her man, her family might refuse to talk to her, to eat at the same table with her, or to buy her clothing, virtually relegating her to the status of house slave. In extreme cases, she might be forced out of the home entirely "so she won't ruin my other daughters." Neighbors might then parrot the family's example, demanding that their own daughters be kept way from this pariah. At the very least, she would be banished from the church and have to make a confession in order to return.

Witnessing just such a public confession when I was twelve contributed in large measure to my view of being "morally good."

The girl's name was Kathy, and the father of her child was long gone. Head bent in shame, she stood before the cold congregation, holding her eighteen-month-old son to her narrow hip, making confession so that her church membership could be restored and she could sing in the choir. I sat tensely, not fully understanding why the girl had to submit to this horrible humiliation and hoping that my daddy or momma or somebody would stand up for her. Nobody did. She stood alone, exposing her sin to a congregation of judges.

I vowed then that no woman was ever going to hurt like that because of me. And if any dude messed up my sister, I'd track him down to the ends of the earth.

All those Valley mores were still with me in St. Louis. Now my self-examination brought me face-to-face with them and with my own suppressed sexual feelings. I recognized that my pre-Bridge impulses had not been burnt out of me as I had supposed; they had just been pushed down by powerful feelings of fear and guilt. Now they were surfacing, pushing for expression. They were the reason I had taken part in the bull sessions and walked through the red-light district. I had hidden behind a cloak of chastity instead of dealing honestly with myself. And while I believed and respected God's commandments about adultery and fornication, my abstinence was due more to fear than to faith. Had it not been for those fears, I knew I would have violated those commandments many times.

One of my fears was that girls would no longer find me sexually desirable. Another was my physical awkwardness: even if a girl was willing, how could I make love to her? Yet I was a young man with normal drives and desires. No matter how much I willed myself not to want sex, my body and my thoughts were gripped by powerful and normal human urges.

That is why I began thinking about prostitutes. If I were ever to have sexual intercourse, I thought, I would probably have to resort to using such a woman. The indignity and immorality they represented, though, helped me realize this, too, was not for me. Were I to use them, I reasoned, I could not pretend to be anything more than an animal.

So my inner conflict continued: pulled by desire . . . rebuked by conscience. I desperately wanted God's way for my life, and this raging turmoil was blocking that objective. I felt dirty and cheap. Even worse, I considered myself an absolute hypocrite. Sometimes it seemed there were two people inside me: one loving God and the other lusting for a woman. This conflict and temptation came close to destroying my faith. Many times I wanted a woman more than I wanted Christ.

"That
Remarkable
Young Man"

"AND NOW, LADIES and gentlemen, we have with us a remarkable young man, brought up from the Mississippi mud . . ." I had heard it over and over again . . . in Baton Rouge, in Little Rock, in Memphis, in St. Louis, in Chicago. Each time I heard it, I had to fight back my resentment. Each time, I cringed, hoping Dr. Mallory would at least skip the rest. But each time she went on and on about the armless boy "who keeps himself clean and immaculately dressed, who is almost a straight-A student, who does all his writing with his mouth. . . ." There were other students who were equally well-dressed and who had grades just as good as mine. She was simply exploiting my handicap. But Dr. Mallory never could understand my feelings.

She had been a pioneer in developing quality education for blacks in Holmes County, Mississippi, with a commitment so deep that she sacrificed everything—even marriage—for her goal. Her dream was to make Saint's a respected, four-year college. To that end she worked tirelessly.

Part of her genius was in raising money. The Church of God in Christ partially subsidized the school, but to make up the deficit, Dr.

126

Mallory constantly engineered fund-raising events. She could talk to anyone, from the most sophisticated to the most simple, the most liberal to the most racist, and always come away with money. Yet she never seemed to mince words or compromise her stand.

Once, in Gloster, Mississippi, I was certain she had gone too far. There she stood, flat-footed and righteous, before an integrated audience, telling them unequivocally what was wrong with society. Then she spoke of Saint's and its role in correcting injustice. My mind flashed back to the previous year when some colored people in Gloster had been severely beaten by whites. But Dr. Mallory knew what she was doing. After she finished, whites in the audience not only applauded generously, but made handsome donations as well.

Now it was the spring of 1951. We were in Milwaukee and the church was jammed with people. The glee club sang "The Lord's Prayer" and Dr. Mallory introduced me. "And now, ladies and gentlemen . . . a remarkable young man. . . ."

"And God stepped out on space and said, 'I'm lonely. I'll make me a world.'" Those were my opening lines; I had learned to deliver them with strength and power. Perhaps because I felt lonely, too—isolated from the other students by Dr. Mallory's exaggerated praise. They would look at me as if to say, "Bud Doggy, is all this really true, man?" I was ashamed to face them.

That night I realized that my days at Saint's were almost over. It had become too dangerous for me to stay, and the danger was double-pronged. First, however ridiculous the praise was, it was difficult not to yield to believing some of it. And second, I needed to know I counted as a person in my own right, not just because of my disability.

When I returned to Saint's after the Milwaukee trip, I talked all this over with Mrs. Booker, who then convened a meeting of my advisors. We agreed I should leave Saint's and finish my preparatory education at Southern Christian Institute in Edwards, Mississippi.

Dr. Mallory was a difficult person to refuse. She genuinely gave of herself and made others feel guilty when they refused her. But if I were to salvage my self-respect, I had to leave.

My years at Saint's had been good ones. God had put Dr. Mallory in my life, and I did not really want to leave her. But I took comfort in the knowledge that all good gifts, while of God, were not God. There was no need to cling to anything but Him.

Preaching
and
Whooping

MY FIRST OPPORTUNITY to preach came that summer after I left Saint's. It was a hot and sultry Sunday night and the Valley View Baptist Church was crowded. Folks had turned out in numbers large enough to scare the devil. The whole Valley seemed to be there—old people too frail for canes, mothers with babies sucking contentedly at their breasts, and young adults lining the walls so their elders could sit. There were also conspicuous non-regulars: the gambler and the bootlegger, the tongue-wagger, the woman-chaser, and the husband-borrower.

"I just had to see with my own two eyes and hear with my own two ears that no-arm boy preach. Them preachers with somethin' wrong can sho-nuff preach, honey. Everybody know what a good preacher Reverend Brown is, and he can't see nary a lick. And the people still talkin' 'bout that peg-leg preacher from up there 'round Greenwood and how he tore up the church that time and had the whole house shoutin'. Chil', I made up my mind when I first heard he was gonna preach, I wasn't gonna let nothin' keep me from comin'."

From my place in the high-backed chair on the platform, I could see Momma and Daddy, Grandma Rushing and Diana, my brothers and sisters—it seemed everyone I knew was there.

After the singing, Deacon Brown got up to introduce me.

"Brothers and sisters," he said, "we have with us tonight one of our own."

"Amen," acknowledged the congregation.

"He is a son of the church, one we done had a hand with."

"Amen," they answered forcefully.

All week long I had practiced diligently and fervently on Prince Edward Hill. I had beaten the magnolia trees into salvation. Excitement welled within me. I had already counted the folks who were going to get happy and shout away. Sister Harris and Sister Wood were pretty easy. No one could make Momma shout, not even Reverend Jackson, but I could count on Grandma. The amens shot up more rapidly as loquacious Deacon Brown expertly primed the tempo.

As I made my way to the pulpit, I scrutinized my audience the way Dr. Mallory had taught me. Here was a live congregation ready to receive the Spirit. The amens subsided so they could hear my opening statement.

"Giving honor to God, Reverend Israel, deacons, members, and friends, I want to thank Deacon Brown for his introduction, and the church for this here glorious opportunity. My text tonight is—" I paused, "from Genesis 6:3. 'And the Lord said, My spirit shall not always strive with man, for that he also is flesh. Yet his days shall be a hundred and twenty years.'" Another pause. "My subject is, 'When the ball is over, somebody gonna die.'"

A few "wells" and "humm-mms" broke the silence. They were warmed up and ready. In fact, between the singing and Deacon Brown's talkathon, the people had gotten a trifle too worked up. The amens swept the church before I properly got started. In my anxiety to preach the house down, I made the mistake of letting the congregation push me too fast. Before I realized it, I had jumped over my preaching and had landed right in the middle of my whoop.

In the Valley, whooping was a preacher's way of shouting while still keeping the message intact. By the time that point was reached, the preacher was in the throes of the Spirit and the congregation was shouting with him. Although the whoop was generally thought to be God-given inspiration, I had practiced mine on Prince Edward Hill just in case. Being unable to whoop was a clear sign you didn't have the Spirit.

I tried to back up in order to work in the preaching, but the congregation wouldn't go for it. They knew you couldn't slam the brakes on the whoop like that. Tradition dictated that when the whoop ended, so did the sermon. It was always the climax. The situation was critical, for the amens began to subside. They were leaving me stranded. I decided to let them have my whoop and bluff it through.

"The son of God is a-comin' back, His eyes a-blazin' like great big balls of hot fire . . . His feet a-shinin' like polished brass . . . His kneebones a-smokin' like a Valley chimney . . . His hair a-bristlin' like lamb's wool. He gonna come back, Bible in one hand, a big, long log-chain in the other. His horse gonna be the wind, and like a ropin' cowboy, He gonna loop the devil's neck and chain him down tight, and y'all who aren't livin' right gonna be chained too, right along with the devil. Then Jesus gonna throw the devil and y'all into an eternally burnin' hell. . . . When the ball is over, somebody gonna die."

By this time only the regular "ameners" were still at it. Everybody else had stopped. I felt desperate and humiliated. If they wanted preaching, I would give it to them. I looked them over, gathering my material. Reverend Douglas was going to hell for staying drunk all the time. Deacon Matthews always winked at the young girls. Miss Jamie wore tight skirts to tempt the men. And Deacon Plummer pulled out a dollar bill as if to put it in the collection plate, then eased it back into his pocket. I knew my audience.

"When the ball is over . . ." I preached it to Sister Banks and Sister Henry, arch-rivals who sat on the same pew each Sunday. "One time, Sister Banks got to shoutin' and took to beatin' Sister Henry with her purse. Sister Henry started packin' an ice pick and was heard to say 'If Sally Banks ever try that trick agin, I gonna ram this here pick in her behind.' When the ball is over, God gonna get them both for sure—one for playin' with the Holy Ghost and the other for seekin' revenge. When the ball is over, somebody gonna die."

I told them how their sins in this life were "gonna plague you beyond the grave and fill all your days beyond eternity. Y'all who wink your eyes at young girls gonna be wearin' a permanent wink. Y'all who shout and ain't got nothin' gonna hafta keep shoutin' all the time. Y'all who pretend to put money in church and don't gonna hafta stand at a table in hell all the time, a-puttin' your hand in and outta your pocket. Y'all who mess with moonshine gonna be drinkin' whiskey every minute through a hose, plugged to a moonshine still for the duration of eternity. You crap shooters gonna hafta pop your fingers raw. When the ball is over, the devil's gonna be gettin' every one of you if you don't straighten up and a-fly right. When the ball is over, somebody gonna die."

Each time I named what they would go to hell for, I lost support. I named everything I could think of, determined to take out my rejection on them. I mixed in a little of the Bible, a little of *Paradise Lost,* a little of *The Divine Comedy,* and a little of *Pilgrim's Progress,* all of which I had read but with precious little understanding. Finally, I got no amens at all. The silence distracted me so that I lost the thread of what I had to say. There was no use pretending any longer. I had more than worn out my welcome. I sat down.

After the service I received bits of encouragement from Pastor Israel, Deacon Brown, and others, but I knew what to think of my performance I had the distinction of being the only preacher in the Valley who had whooped before he had preached.

When I got home, Momma saw how crestfallen I was. "Bud Doggy, people don't like for preachers just to tell them what's wrong," she said. "They wanta know what's good about them, too. Folks got a lotta problems and they want to be told how God's love gonna lift them up and not just how his punishment gonna whup them down. But whenever you done preach what the Lawd hisself done give you to preach, you shouldn't feel bad. If you preachin' what the Lawd want you to preach, you ain't gotta worry about how people feel about you. The thing you gotta be sure about is that you is preachin' what he done give you to preach."

Momma's words pricked my spirit. I saw that my preaching had very little to do with God's will. I had been vain and full of pride, concerned only about the impression I was making. And when I had not succeeded as I hoped, I got angry. I understood my guilt and prayed for forgiveness.

"Lord, I have used your pulpit and have turned your Word to say my own feelings. Please forgive me, Lord. Please give me more love and patience. I want to be the right kind of good preacher, Lord. I want to help folks the way you told me to. I know you love me, and I know you have called me to preach your Word, but I see I can't do it my way."

Real
Friendship

THAT FALL, 1951, when I was almost nineteen, I entered Southern Christian Institute, a campus of twelve buildings isolated on four hundred acres of rolling land in rural Mississippi. The small town of Edwards stood 2 miles away, historical Vicksburg 15 miles away, and the Valley 120 miles away.

SCI was a serious institution with a long, proud history. Its faculty, mostly white and well-trained, was a dedicated group that gave the school a reputation for a stiff curriculum. Each teacher was a specialist in his or her particular area, though the school was only a junior college.

SCI was run under the auspices of the Christian Church (Disciples of Christ), and the church and the faith were a strong force in the lives of both faculty and the three hundred students. In contrast to Saint's, the Bible was not quoted constantly; yet it was felt in operation. The students, who were largely from the rural South, the urban North, and the Carribbean, came from various denominational backgrounds. However, denominational and regional differences were dwarfed by the spirit of fellowship and freedom which the school fostered; the love of Christ was evident and active in the lives of teachers and students.

At that time in my life, SCI was just the right place for me. Not since Forty-Four had I been under the influence of a strong, black male figure. Not since Diana had I felt accepted and loved by a girl. And not since Bubba had I experienced true friendship. At SCI, Jesse James Hawkins, Bernice Charles, and the gang of seven satisfied all those needs.

Jesse James Hawkins, my psychology teacher (we called him "The Hawk" in his absence) was small, but a man of remarkable courage. None of us would challenge him. From Forty-Four I had learned the value of standing up for my rights. From the Coxes I had learned the value of Christian love. From Dr. Mallory I had learned the value of scholarship. But Jesse James taught me the importance of standing up for my convictions. He taught me racial loyalty and that to live a lie only hurt myself and my people. When anyone, black or white or whatever, threatened the dignity of black people, Jesse James would tighten up and fight like the bandit he was named after. I admired him and learned from him the value of self-respect and respect for black people, both men and women.

Bernice Charles was a twenty-year-old, honey-brown, studious, advanced freshman. She was not slender like the girls I was typically attracted to, but seductive and stoutly built, with bright, flashing eyes that kept my attention. Bernice seized command of our relationship from the start, and never turned loose. I couldn't get her to "dance to my music," and I couldn't get myself to stop dancing to hers. I was almost kicked out of SCI when the matron caught us in the midst of a prolonged kiss. We were put on probation and warned that we'd better behave. The relationship eventually waned, but I was always the richer for having known her. It was not Bernice's kisses or loveliness or intelligence that influenced me; it was the self-esteem she gave me by both her affection and her presence in my life. She accepted me as a whole man, still attractive to the opposite sex. She gave me back my self-confidence and self-esteem in that regard.

When I first arrived at SCI, social functions still intimidated me. I invented excuse after excuse to ease my withdrawal from such activities:

135

"I don't like dances." "Cookout food gripes my stomach." "I get red bugs at picnics." I learned to fake illness, timing it well in advance of an event. In time, my rationalizations became even more sophisticated. I could fabricate reasons on the spot and at the same time intimidate others with my piety. I squared this with my conscience by declaring that dances were frivolous and sinful and rattled off the Scriptures to back me up. "Sicking one on the Bible" was a technique of quoting, or more often misquoting, the Scriptures to prove yourself right. I became a master at it.

Though my behavior caused some to hold me in awe, it stifled friendships with my fellow students. While I was respected and often admired, I was not truly loved. I was left to pump my own lonely way up life's road, oblivious to what I really wanted. I did not understand what a stressful toll this was taking or how desperately I needed the friendship of others until I learned what real friendship was.

Real friendship came in the form of seven of my SCI classmates— Renetta, Velma, Joyce, Maude, Carolyn, Ledell, and Tommy. They were an exciting bunch, academically motivated, aware of what they wanted in life, with a sound perspective on life and truth. Providentially, I fell into this group and became one of them. Each of us had a role: Renetta was the intellectual; Joyce and Velma were the promoters; Carolyn was the stylist; Ledell was the fixer; Tommy was the stabilizer; Maude was the swing voter; and I became the strategist. We ran our class and wanted to run the school—and probably would have if The Hawk had allowed us to. We accepted, trusted, and relied on each other. If one had a need, all felt its blow and moved collectively to meet it. With the seven I experienced a form of sharing and fraternity I had not known since Bubba.

Commencement would put an end to all this, of course. We would graduate, go home for the summer, and then go to different colleges in the fall. Our friendship would become a casualty of that which we had worked so hard to achieve.

Leaving those newly found and desperately needed friends created an ache from which I doubted I could ever recover, but the experience also led me to an important discovery about the passage of things: We live just long enough to get a slight taste of history. We realize that friendships, feelings, institutions, everything we are involved in, are constantly in transition, no matter how permanent they may appear when we are young. Miss Judy, Bubba, Diana, the Wire, the hospital, the bridge, the Coxes, Saint's, SCI, and all the other significant influences in my life, even sickness and death, were but fleeting moments. They came, tarried, and passed away. Only the eternal moment of God would last forever. So there was no need to worry about the past. My task was to prepare for those moments ahead of me.

When commencement came, I thanked God for the prospects of my future which now seemed brighter and brighter.

Stillman
College

THE TRAILWAYS BUS sped through twisting hills, leaving the black soil of the Mississippi Delta and rolling toward the red clay of eastern Mississippi and Alabama. Another school was behind me, another summer gone. At last I was on my way to college. Stately oaks and pines dotting the hillsides blurred through the windows. Occasionally, smoke wafting from a gully betrayed houses hidden among the trees. From time to time we zipped past ante-bellum homes sitting aloof on spacious lawns, protectively cradled by rows of majestic trees.

This was my first trip through eastern Mississippi, but towns I had read about in history books rolled by, making the landscape seem familiar and friendly. When we passed Starksville, home of Mississippi State University, I found myself admiring the buildings and envying the students who strolled the grounds so complacently. *You're not allowed there,* I thought. *Unless you're going to do something about it, don't admire it.* And something like a chill went through me.

When we reached Tuscaloosa, I got off the bus and took a cab to West Tuscaloosa. There, nestled meekly on a hill high above the Warrior River, was Stillman College, the place in which I had invested so much hope. At first glance, it was disappointing. I suppose because the idea of college had grown so large in my mind, I expected the college to be large. Out of the eight buildings clustered together on 120 acres, only one of them, Cocrane Hall, looked collegiate enough to command my respect. The rest of the campus was an assortment of carefully preserved homes, tenements, and small shops. Obviously Stillman's building program was ruled more by practicality than aesthetics.

I paused in the shade of magnolias to admire Cocrane Hall, reputed to have been a plantation house built by slaves. It rested on six giant pillars adorned with elegant Corinthian columns imported from Italy. Black folks had built it; finally they had the use of it. I would soon learn that this magnificent old building was to be replaced by a more practical facility. I could only hope it would last through my years there.

However, I quickly dismissed my feelings of disappointment, and within two hours I was filing into the gym with ninety-two other freshmen for orientation. We learned about the layout of the campus, the history of the college, and an impressive list of dos and don'ts while faculty members and students assessed each other.

Soon, I became aware that someone was watching me intently—a tall, stately woman in her middle forties. The silver of her graying hair contrasted with her simple black dress and highlighted her aristocratic good looks.

After the orientation, she came over and laid her gentle, white hand on my shoulder. "I'm Myrtle Williamson," she said. "I'm so glad you chose to come to Stillman."

"Thank you very much, ma'am."

Kindness mapped her features, but it was her eyes that arrested me and gripped me all the while we were chatting. When I left, I could feel them following me. Somehow I felt those eyes were God's eyes and that He was promising they would look after me here.

Campus religious life was dominated by Miss Myrtle Williamson. She was a wholehearted Presbyterian who loved the church, people, and Stillman. Her lifestyle was saintly and ascetic. She craved neither wealth nor power, hated no one, and gave a large portion of her income to the needy.

At first it was difficult for me to believe that any human being, particularly a white one, could be as pure and innocent and good as Miss Williamson seemed to be. I did my best to find something wrong in her to justify my skepticism. But her goodness finally won me over, and I spent many hours with her discussing Christian living, church doctrine, segregation, and my own Christian vocation and commitment. Under her tutelage I attended various ecumenical conferences and read books dealing with social problems.

Miss Williamson's gift for loving and accepting all kinds of people impressed me tremendously. Praying for Dr. Martin Luther King and the civil rights movement was one thing; but when she suggested that we pray for Governor Orville Faubus and Governor Ross Barnett, the segregationists, I froze, unable to continue. Something inside would not allow it. How could any Christian pray for segregationists when God himself was against segregation?

"They are God's children, too, Phillip," Miss Williamson said.

"But they are real bad children, ma'am," I countered.

Nevertheless, it was this undiscriminating love I had seen in her eyes on orientation day; it was this love that had drawn me to her—the kind of love to which her whole life was a witness.

It was Miss Myrtle Williamson's love and encouragement that inspired me to become a campus leader. In my freshman year I was elected president of my class. In my sophomore year I was elected campus Sunday school superintendent. In my junior year I was elected president of the men's dormitory.

Many students, however, resented my association with Miss Williamson. They were annoyed by her efforts to make them into better Christians, and they thought I was too much of a disciple of "that white woman."

All my time at Stillman was not devoted to studies and spirituality, of course. That first day outside Cocrane Hall, I had met a grinning, bony, six-foot son of a Methodist minister from Alabama, Leonard Holmes, who became my closest friend at Stillman.

It was Leonard who got me into the business of advising guys on how to handle their girl problems. Reserved and especially shy with girls, Leonard told me with mock seriousness how much he relied upon my advice to keep him out of trouble. But others took him seriously and began coming to me for help. Even after my reputation was established and I valued my counseling services at twenty-five cents per session, they kept coming. Soon I had developed a profitable little enterprise that provided extra spending money.

The counselor himself didn't get seriously involved with anyone on campus. I had already loved and lost twice. But I had my own neurotic little trick with the girls: it was important to get them romantically interested in me so that I could then reject them on the basis of my holiness. This guaranteed that I would never feel neglected or undesirable.

More
Open
Doors

THE SUMMER BEFORE my senior year, 1956, I entered a subscription-selling contest sponsored by *Time-Life* publications. My goal was to win first prize, a tape recorder, which I would use to help improve my speech. My sponsors would have provided one for me if I had asked, but it seemed important that I earn it myself. So daily I hitchhiked the thirty miles from the Valley to Greenwood and went knocking door-to-door.

At first I confined myself to the homes of poor colored folks. They received me warmly, glad to have some distraction from the monotony of their existence. Inside those depressing shacks, bright-eyed, syrup-fingered children watched me above their plates of bread and molasses; soon their sticky fingers followed their eyes, dirtying my clean shirt. I endured these inspections as patiently as I could, but the little ones often distracted the parent from my discourse and, on more than one occasion, killed my sale.

As I moved into the more affluent colored section, I discovered that even the greatest patience did nothing to soften the impact of doors slammed in my face. Trying to reassure myself that the rejection was not personal, I trudged along and persisted. If folks listened, I talked. And if

142

I talked long enough, they bought. I even found ways of winning over the unfriendly ones. If they held me at bay through their screen doors, I played hard-of-hearing, getting them to crack the door. Then I kept the door ajar with my foot and talked strongly and earnestly until they finally let me in. I made sales in seven out of ten houses I entered.

With only two days left in the contest, I needed thirty additional sales. My daily volume had never exceeded ten orders, so I knew I needed a new market, and fast. I had to get to people who read and had money. That meant white folks.

I had avoided white folks in my sales plan for two reasons: I was colored, and white folks usually kept dogs around their houses. While the dogs were not a fearful obstacle, just a nuisance, the thought of knocking on the doors of white folks' houses did cause me some trepidation. Just a few miles from Greenwood, a black man named Emmet Till had been lynched for allegedly whistling at a white woman. Of course, my armlessness did give me an advantage: white folks could hardly accuse me of coming to steal or to molest their women. So I figured I was safe as long as I didn't whistle!

The next day I tried out my new prospects without telling anyone, because I knew Momma would worry. When I stepped up to the first door, the right words came.

"I'm Bud Doggy from the Valley Plantation," I began. "Mr. Buford is the owner. I'm a college student, and God has called me to preach. I don't talk too plain, and I need a tape recorder to help improve my speech. To win one, I got to make thirty sales in the next two days. What will your subscription be, ma'am?" Then I took my pencil from my shirt pocket with my mouth and proceeded to write up the order.

I repeated this routine often in the next two days. Amazingly, I negotiated forty-two orders the first day and fifty-four the next. I made a sale at every house I visited. One man paid the $7.50 for the magazine with a twenty-dollar bill and said, "Keep the change, boy." I thanked him, but refused. I recognized him as the owner of the large feed company I had gone to many times with Mr. Harold.

"Perhaps, sir," I said, "you might want to buy subscriptions for your employees?" He seemed mildly shocked at the suggestion, but quickly agreed and bought twenty subscriptions. The next day I told the owner of the oil mill what Mr. Roberts had done and succeeded in getting thirty subscriptions for his employees.

The Lord of abundance had smiled down on His son's determination. I won the tape recorder and earned six hundred dollars in commissions. This was an important experience for me, for I realized I would never have to go hungry. I was a good salesman; I could earn my own way. I might not have arms, but the Lord had given me a good mind and had enabled me to learn how to use my mouth. As long as I had those, other hands would open the doors for me, just as God had promised that day on the bridge.

One day as I was doing my door-to-door routine with the downtown merchants, I noticed a white man standing in front of the bank. His felt hat angled sharply, nearly hiding his right eye, but I could tell he was watching me. I watched him, too, trying not to be obvious. His expensive mohair suit and relaxed posture implied money and authority.

Why was he watching me? In the Valley, white folks of consequence were much too busy with their own activities to watch colored folks, even colored folks they thought might rip them off. They hired poor whites to watch for them. This man's preoccupation with me made me nervous. I suppressed a powerful urge to walk up to him and ask, "Okay, white folks, what's on your mind?" That would have been asking for trouble, perhaps even the rope.

I finished working Johnson Street and made my way up Carrollton, making sure I walked right by him.

"Pardon me, boy," he said as I drew near, "what's your name?"

I looked at him straight. "Bud Doggy, sir."

"How did you get a name like that?"

"Forty-Four gave it to me, sir."

He leaned forward slightly. "Who?"

"Forty-four. My granddaddy."

"I guess you saw me watching you."

"No, sir," I lied, remembering Forty-Four's advice to steer clear of entanglements with whites.

"I'm Robert Jones. I know President Hay at Stillman well, and I believe you are the boy he mentioned to me and Reverend Duncan. He spoke very admiringly of you, and after seeing your efforts, I can't help but marvel at your guts. What are you selling?"

"Magazine subscriptions, sir."

"How is it going?"

"Fine, sir. My goal is to win a tape recorder to help me when I go back to Stillman."

"Good school, Stillman, good school. Doing a good job educating colored boys and girls over there. You like it there, do you?"

"Oh, yes, sir. I can hardly wait till the vacation is over." I thought I knew how to talk to *them*.

"Well, before you go back, stop in to see me." He pulled a business card from his pocket, crossed out his office address, and penned in the name of Greenwood's largest Presbyterian church. He then put the card in my pocket. "Next Wednesday at ten, then, how's that?"

"Fine, sir," I said, wondering what he really wanted.

Promptly at ten the following Wednesday, I pushed open the carved oak door of the Presbyterian church. I had never been in a white people's church before. I was dazzled by the sun pouring through the stained-glass windows. The secretary greeted me warmly and as if she was expecting me. She told me that Mr. Jones was out but that Reverend Duncan would talk to me.

The sandy-haired Reverend Duncan soon ushered me into his office. "Good morning, Bud Doggy. I'm Reverend Duncan." He reached out his hand, then quickly drew it back.

I smiled. "It's okay, sir, just shake my sleeve."

I looked around his office. Behind the huge mahogany desk were cases and cases of books. I wondered if he had read them all. The secretary brought in two ice-cold Cokes, and Reverend Duncan seemed stunned when I took mine between my teeth, held it aloft, and drank without spilling a drop.

I felt the need to put him at ease. "Thanks for the Coke, Reverend Duncan, and for the air conditioning, too. It's really hot today."

He nodded amiably and began the conversation in earnest. "Mr. Jones is interested in you, Bud Doggy." Then he asked about my grades, and I told him I had made the honor roll every quarter. He asked about my plans, and I told him I wanted to be a counseling minister. Reverend

Duncan listened closely to all I said, complimented me on my grades, and told me that he thought the ministry was a wonderful profession and a good choice for me.

After about forty-five minutes, he indicated that our talk was over. "Bud Doggy, I feel certain Mr. Jones will want to see you himself." He gave me an appointment for the following Tuesday and wished me Godspeed and success. I left, still not knowing what the two men were up to.

The following Tuesday, Mr. Jones awaited me in the same study. He spoke with a calm authority that indicated long acquaintance with power.

"Reverend Duncan speaks very highly of your accomplishments. We both admire your courage—the way you were working out there on the streets the other day. By the way, how did it go?"

I told him that I had achieved my major objectives for the summer; I had earned six hundred dollars and won the tape recorder.

"Incredible . . . incredible," he repeated, as though talking to himself. "And you did all your writing with your mouth . . . incredible."

He then sat up and spoke more firmly and directly. "The Lord has blessed me with considerable wealth. I guess I'm one of the wealthiest men around here. One of the pleasures of having money is to be able to support causes I feel strongly about. I support Stillman College through the church. I like what they're doing. Now I want to do something for you. What do you need?"

"Nothing really, Mr. Jones. I'll buy my school clothes with the money I made this summer. My educational expenses are already taken care of."

"I'll tell you what . . . I want you to help your brothers and sisters with that money, and I'm going to pay for your clothes." He then scribbled a note, sealed it in an envelope, and instructed me to take it to Mr. George, the owner of one of the town's leading men's stores.

I thanked Mr. Jones and left, but suspicion and curiosity made that letter red-hot in my pocket. I did not know what to make of such altruism, especially from these white men who hardly knew me. Though it wasn't really mail, I felt it was wrong for me to read the note. Then I remembered Uriah in the Old Testament—he got done in because he didn't read his note. I detoured into a restaurant where I put my curi-

146

osity to rest. The note read: "George, give this boy what he wants, and bill me."

At the store I picked out an inexpensive suit, a shirt, and a tie. Mr. George protested, "Is that all? Mr. Jones wants you to have more than that, I'm sure." He made a phone call and came back smiling. "Mr. Jones wants you to get at least three suits of quality," he said.

My senior year I returned to Stillman with a tape recorder, a new wardrobe, and plenty of spending money. I felt ten feet tall, sharp as a razor, and prouder than a Valley peacock.

Commencement

MY LAST YEAR at Stillman was not a peaceful one. The civil rights movement had been growing in the nation. As its effects began to be felt, it involved both the school and myself in bitter controversy.

Stillman invited the University of Alabama's nationally recognized debate team to our campus. Just before the scheduled appearance, Alabama became embroiled in criticism because of the treatment of Autherine Lucy, their first black student. Stillman students wanted the invitation withdrawn. The administration refused to cancel. They also refused to allow Dr. Martin Luther King to speak on our campus. I felt Stillman had knuckled under the pressure of white folks and the school's more conservative supporters, and this provoked a terrible bitterness in me.

I had not felt such rage since the anguish prior to my conversion six years before. It ravaged my powers of reason and love. I wanted to hate anything that even looked white. I castigated my white professors and accused them of racism. I criticized my quiet-mouthed, black professors as "Uncle Toms." Even my relationship with Miss Williamson grew sour.

With tears in her eyes, she said, "Phillip, you have a streak of meanness in you that is frightening."

My Momma had told me that, and so had Diana, but I figured I had traveled a long way from my beloved family and friends in the Valley, folks who wished they had not been born black. Folks who hotcombed their hair to straighten out the kinks and loaded their faces with "Black and White" bleaching cream. Folks who believed The Man when he told them how little they were worth.

My fury grew so intense that I almost jeopardized everything I had worked for. Stillman had a no-nonsense church attendance policy, and I made it the focal point of my resistance. I would not attend any church that white folks had anything to do with. I was given a strong warning, but still refused to attend. Finally I was brought before the disciplinary committee, where I was told I either had to fall in line or leave. I fell in line.

Part of my problem was that I could see my own inconsistency, and that I, too, was vulnerable to fear—and also to hatred, pride, and prejudice. The college administration had refused to cancel the debate team's invitation because they feared endangering an arrangement that would enable Stillman to benefit from the University's leading professors. They had refused to invite Dr. King because they feared antagonizing members of the church who controlled the school's finances. I had caved in because I feared what the school could do to me. Though I still thought the school was wrong, I knew I could not judge them without judging myself.

It took a good six months to work myself through this dilemma. During that time, Miss Williamson never ceased loving me and doing for me, and eventually our relationship was once again warm and trusting.

Those six months during my senior year were in some ways as important as all the rest of my education combined, for it was through that experience that I began to put together all my feelings about the plantation system, the white man, the black man, and myself. I had already had experiences which made me value my blackness. I had been to places where the races mixed. I knew whites whom I loved and respected; I knew whites who loved and respected me. I would never have learned about human equality from The Man, but I would never have learned it from my family either, for they were as brainwashed and defeated by the system as he was.

I was light years away from the system I had left, simply because I could choose. The Valley, with its non-thinking apathy, its bitterness and sloth, its passion and futility were passing away from me. I now understood the plantation system, The Man who ran it, the folks who lived under it, and the underlying fear that connected them. One was the persecutor and the other the victim, yet neither lived God's love. Instead, they deceived themselves into believing they had a cause for doing what they did, while ignoring the First Cause who had created them all in His image and for His glory.

Stillman College had been good to me, in spite of my fling with rebellion. I completed my studies, and finally sat with my classmates— like myself, older and wiser—at the commencement exercises in a filled Birthright Auditorium.

The commencement speaker was Dr. Albert C. Wynn, a scholarly redneck who was an outstanding teacher, a Christian gentlemen, and a most impressive preacher. He was the first white minister I met who knew the difference between preaching and reading a sermon. Though his reputation would have easily secured him a professorship at a better-known institution, he had chosen Stillman.

His closing words have never ceased living in me: "When you go back to your communities, you will be more educated than others. But your degree is not to be worn as a badge of pride. It is a license to serve. To him who has received much . . . of him much is required."

As I sat there reflecting on the implication of what Dr. Wynn had said, I heard my name called from the stage.

"Rushing, Phillip Van . . . *magna cum laude.*"

I rose to receive, that someday I might be able to give.

After

The Blessing
of
the Wire

IN MARCH, 1958, at the age of twenty-six, I left the Valley for Lexington Seminary in Lexington, Kentucky. As I boarded the Greyhound and settled into a window seat with a last view of Tchula, Mississippi, I also looked back on all that had happened to me.

Nine Christmases before I had lost my arms. Other passengers now stared at the evidence of this—the metallic hooks peeping from beneath my jacket sleeves. I could bear to be stared at now. Sometimes I stared at myself, praising God and reflecting on how His grace could reconstruct an entire being from within.

As I relaxed in the high-cushioned seat and looked at the metal hooks extending from my new set of plastic limbs, I thought of the less-than-optimistic report from the manufacturer of my artificial arms. Other than cosmetic benefits, I was not to expect to derive much use from them. Yet within two days of having them, I had learned to use my new hands to feed myself and had written a letter to Momma in my very first effort. The maker of the limbs knew their limitations; my Maker knew their possibilities. And I knew Him. Faith in Him produced extraordinary results.

"Of all sad words of tongue and pen, the saddest are these: it might have been." To me, the meaning of those words was simple and literal, not a nostalgia for the past. There was a life much worse than an armless life. Life without love or respect. Life without spirituality or integrity. Life without freedom or faith. Life without hope or purpose. Any or all of these were infinitely sadder than life without arms. Such lives were symptoms of the one cause of all human suffering and humiliation—life without God.

Before the Wire, I had been poised on the brink of just such a life. *Where would I be today if the Wire hadn't burned away part of me that December day,* I wondered.

I might have stayed in the Valley, stayed loyal to the plantation system, as my father had. The pull of the plantation could have had me before I knew it. The toil of the Valley squeezed out the spirit of life. Descendants of bronze kings and black giants surrendered dignity and soul just to survive there. No one could battle it and win. Most of my family had lost themselves to it.

Perhaps Diana and I would have married. The Valley would have sneaked into us, just as it had to Momma and Daddy. We would have made plans to leave and then postponed them when the first baby came. Then there would be another baby, another year, and our enthusiasm for leaving would have worn thin. After depending on The Man for so long, we'd be lost without him to manage things—to look out for us, to think for us, to tell us what to do. So we'd stay on, neither of us willing to admit that the Valley fear had finally clawed into us. So we'd keep talking about how one day we were just going to pull up stakes and haul off. Just turn-row talking.

I would have watched Diana grow bent and passive, just like Momma. And I would have grown dull and submissive, just like Daddy.

Or, I might have recognized that I had to get away. I might have sold the cow and the hog, kissed Diana good-by, and boarded "The City of New Orleans" train to take me as far north as my ticket would allow, promising to send for her later. But after the Valley had marked me, mere flight was not enough. Drained of energy, numb to love and the ability to think, what good is freedom? When you are told all your life what to do and what not to do, how many acres to work and what to plant, what mule to plow and which plow to use, what time to go to the field and when to come in, what barbershop to use and which doctor to visit, how many groceries to buy and which merchant to buy from, what church to attend and what graveyard to be buried in, there is only one thing left to do by and for yourself . . . to die, one way or another.

I couldn't truly know what I would have done had my sleeves not become empty, but very likely I would have wound up like the others who had left the Valley. Hundreds of country boys before me had done so. I knew some of them—boys with whom I had gone to school, worked in the fields, skipped church, and run errands. Most of them had grown up fast and hard.

Paul Banks got life for robbery.

Isaiah Smith was stabbed to death in bed by his stepdaughter.

Billy Henson was shot dead during an alley crap game.

Doug Johnson died from an overdose of drugs.

Teddy Benson was shot dead by his woman in a Chicago housing project.

Walter Douglas was unemployed, his wife and five children on welfare.

John Pate was unemployed and bitter, having lost his wife to a white man.

Jesse Dee was a wino begging on Chicago's skid row.

B. V. Brown was sunk in alcohol.

Would Bubba have turned out like the others if he had lived? I wondered. *Would I have been like them?* I could have been, and quite possibly would have been—except for the Wire and the grace of God.

Thank You, Lord, for these empty sleeves.

Phillip Rushing

APPROXIMATELY TWENTY-FIVE YEARS have passed since Phillip Rushing's days at Lexington Seminary. After a year in the seminary, he began his career as a social worker. While working full-time in secular employment, he pastored a church, and continued to do that wherever he went—in Kentucky, Mississippi, Illinois, and other places.

His first job in social work was at Kentucky Village, five miles from Lexington, where he worked as a counselor with sixty young, male inmates; he evaluated their rehabilitation and decided whether to recommend parole. Forty percent of his clients were white and most were from the mountains of Kentucky where it was unusual to see a black man in authority.

In 1961 Phillip moved to Chicago to study under a scholarship from the University of Chicago's School of Social Work. In Chicago he took a job as a management aide for the Chicago Housing Authority. His duty station was the Robert R. Taylor Homes, CHA's newest, largest, and most publicized housing project—twenty-eight residential highrises covering fourteen city blocks in length and two in width, housing 28,000 people. It was there that he saw the other side of the dream of many blacks to head north—he saw the reality that the dreams sometimes became nightmares.

As the civil rights movement blossomed into full-scale social revolution, Phillip felt he could not stay in distant Chicago when so many important things were happening back in his native Mississippi. Over the next few years he served the people there in a number of capacities: he was appointed coordinator of the election campaign for the Freedom Democratic Party and worked with the civil rights movement in Holmes County; he helped elect the first black to the Mississippi House of Representatives; he served as Chief Counselor in a Community Action Program in Winona, Mississippi, where his work was so successful that he was recognized with a special citation by the Department of Labor.

Later he returned to Chicago where he worked with a number of community agencies. His most challenging experience during this time was his involvement in mediating a dispute between the Black Panthers and the Black Student Organization. His career continued to develop along the lines of social service and peacemaking, and he was eventually appointed Director of Program Strategy for the Illinois Regional Medical Program.

In 1970, Phillip was awarded an HEW fellowship, one of ten people selected from a field of 15,000 candidates. This recognition took him to suburban Washington D.C. where he became a Special Assistant to the Commissioner of the Health Services and Mental Health Administration. The fellowship lasted one year, and upon its completion he was offered a senior-level position with the government. Instead, he elected to return to his work in Chicago, where in 1972 he became Director of Human Relations for the Illinois Department of Public Aid.

In 1975 he again went to Washington D.C. and remained there until 1978 as Deputy Equal Opportunity Officer for the Food and Drug Administration.

At present, 1984, Phillip Van Rushing is back in Chicago working on his Th.D. at Chicago Theological Seminary. He is married to Mildred Ann Parks and they have four children: Milton, 22, Phillip, 20, Searcy, 18, and Phyllis Ann, 12.